knit mittens!

15 Cool Patterns to Keep You Warm

ROBIN HANSEN

STOREY
BOOKS

The mission of Storey Publishing is to serve our customers by publishing
practical information that encourages personal independence
in harmony with the environment.

Edited by Gwen Steege, Susan Huxley, Cindy Nicholls, and Karen Levy
Designed by Susi Oberhelman
Cover photograph by Giles Prett
Photographs by Robin Holland
Illustrations by Alison Kolesar
Text production by Jennifer Jepson Smith and Jen Rork
Indexed by Susan Olason

Copyright © 2002 by Robin Orm Hansen

Printed in China by C&C Offset Printing Co., Ltd.
10 9 8 7 6 5 4 3 2 1

Library of Congress Cataloging-in-Publication Data
Hansen, Robin Orm.
Knit mittens! : 15 cool patterns to keep you warm / Robin Orm Hansen.
p. cm.
Includes index.
ISBN 1-58017-483-3
1. Knitting—Patterns. 2. Mittens. I. Title.
TT825 .H258 2002
746.43'20432—dc21
2002008709

Contents

Warm Hands, Warm Heart   4

Stop-and-Go Mittens   16

Polar Bear Mitts   22

Lillemor's Mittens   28

Chicky Feet Mittens   34

Fleur-de-Lis Mittens   40

Kid's Fulled Mittens   46

Skier's Finger Mitts   52

Chipman's Block   62

Peek-a-Boo Mittens   70

Covered with Colors   78

Nepalese Mittens   86

Labrador Diamonds   92

Fisherman's Rib   100

Wristers   108

North Star Mittens   114

Index   126

Warm Hands,
Warm Heart

You won't find mittens like these in the big clothing chains or fancy dress shops, or even in sporting goods stores. Good, warm wool mittens are one of the hold-outs from our great-grandmothers' day, something never successfully manufactured either in America or anywhere else in the world. The only way to get great mittens today, as a century ago, is to talk someone into making them for you or to make them yourself.

And make them you can — even if you have felt overwhelmed by inscrutable abbreviations or unexplained techniques before. If you can knit at all, I will sit beside you through directions for some of the niftiest mittens on the continent, which you will then own, in body and spirit, and will be able to make again and again for everyone you care about. Most of these mittens have been passed down through generations, but some are new looks at old ideas. They're good, solid mittens — fun, warm, and, for the most part, easy to make. Try them! When you have made a pair, you will wear them, and you will discover just how good some old ideas can be.

Getting Started

Many handcrafts require a big investment in tools and equipment, along with a hobby room or studio to contain them. And most handcrafts don't travel well, because either the equipment or the materials are messy, big, dangerous, wet, poisonous, or noisy.

Knitting is different: Knitting is peaceful and portable, inexpensive and nonpolluting. All you really need in order to knit is knitting needles, yarn, a place to sit, and a willingness to try. Even avid knitters need little more. They may have collections of knitting needles and boxes full of yarn, but when they sit down to knit, it is little more than that — yarn, needles, and the excitement about what is to come.

A Cheerful Yarn

All of these mittens are knitted with sheep's wool or fibers from another animal — llamas, goats, or rabbits. The two fulled mittens (pages 22 and 46) cannot even be produced with yarn from a plant or synthetic fiber, because they're knitted extra large and rely on the ability of wool to shrink and mat. But that's good: Wool is the warmest fiber in the world, and it's the only fiber that actually keeps you warm when it's wet. When synthetic mittens get wet, they soak and don't easily dry; when wool mittens get damp, the wool pulls together within each fiber and absorbs the wetness. A wool mitten can be quite wet before it actually feels wet. When it is, fling out your arm and shake your hand: Water sprays out in an arc, and the mitten is again damp but toasty.

Whatever yarn you buy, make sure you have enough of each color (and dye lot!) for your project. That may sound strange for such small projects, but the adult sizes can easily go into a second skein in single-color mittens, and if you plan to make more than one pair, you may get stuck with half a mitten less than you planned and no way to buy more yarn in a color that matches exactly. Gather your yarn in consultation with the yarn consumption figures accompanying each pattern. It's better to have yarn left over than not to have enough.

If the yarn store winds the yarn into balls for you, wait until you're ready to start the last skein of each color before having it wound, as unopened skeins can usually be returned or exchanged.

Yarns: Your Choice

Although we tell you what yarn was used for each mitten in the book, you can substitute any yarn that knits comfortably at the same tension (see page 7 for advice about tension).

A Colorful Mix

For this collection of mittens, I've selected colors that make me smile. You are, of course, free to use the same colors or to choose other colors that inspire you. Some people prefer to knit in natural sheep's colors; others like rich, deep, tweedy colors. No matter what your taste, choosing colors is a playground. Enjoy the selection or experiment with your own combinations. The Stop-and-Go mittens (page 16) use yarn dyed in the microwave with Kool-Aid. (See "Colors from the Kitchen," page 21.)

Needle Knowledge

Most of the mittens in this book are knitted "in-the-round," which means you use four double-point needles to knit in a continuous spiral. If you are buying knitting needles only for a particular project and from a congenial shop owner, you might ask if you can knit a test swatch in the store to see if you actually knit at the recommended gauge with that size needle. This could save you from having to buy several sets of needles for a single project.

Spruce, bamboo, aluminum, steel, or plastic — which is best for knitting mittens? Well, it depends. If you are a beginning knitter and are concerned about dropping stitches, you might try wooden or bamboo knitting needles, which are light and stiff but hold onto the stitches well. If you are an experienced knitter, you already know that shiny, coated, metal needles are the fastest in small needle sizes. For needle sizes larger than #8, bamboo or plastic is better, as large metal needles are ungainly and heavy. Knitters with arthritic fingers often like the gentleness and slight give of wooden needles.

The needle sizes in this book are given in American standard (US) and metric sizes. Here are the equivalents for metric and UK/Canadian needle sizes you may need to know for the mittens. Notice that some metric sizes have no US or Canadian equivalent.

US	Metric	UK/Canadian
1	2¼mm	13
	2½mm	
2	2¾mm	12
	3mm	11
3	3¼mm	10
4	3½mm	
5	3¾mm	9
6	4mm	8
7	4½mm	7
8	5mm	6
9	5½mm	5
10	6mm	4
10½	6½mm	3

A Tension, Please!

The important thing about needle size is that needle and yarn sizes regulate the number of stitches you knit per inch — the tension, or gauge, of your knitting. When knitting patterns are set up, the sizes are determined by the knitting tension. You must knit the same number of stitches per inch as the recommended gauge to achieve the same finished measurements and the size you want.

Some knitters will tell you never to knit anything without making a test swatch — a little square more than 2 inches wide made with the same needles, pattern, and yarn as your project. I won't tell you that, since some mittens themselves are barely that wide. For the purposes of mitten knitting only, consider your mitten as a swatch with a thumb, and use that to check the tension.

Knit the cuff with the recommended needle size for the ribbing. Ribbing can be a little tight or loose without the sky falling. When you get to the stockinette portion of the mitten, knit about 1 inch in the pattern and with the suggested needle size, then knit halfway around, and stop. Move the stitches around on the needles so they seem uncrowded and relaxed. Gently flatten out the piece on a smooth surface.

Using a metal needle gauge/ruler, line up the widthwise leg with the very bottom points of a row of stitches and the vertical leg exactly along the edge of a line of stitches. Count either one side of the stitches or the points until you get to 1 inch. If it's doesn't exactly line up with the inch mark, keep counting and see whether it comes out even at 2 inches. If you do not get exactly the gauge called for, try a couple of other locations on the mitten, avoiding spots with thumb gore increases. If you don't have the correct gauge anywhere, rip back to the round above the cuff and reknit on different size needles. Don't just change needles in midstream.

If you have too many stitches per 2 inches, try a larger size needle. If you have too few, try a smaller needle. I find that each US needle size changes the gauge by about half a stitch in either direction.

Checking tension

Stocking Up

You shouldn't buy more needles than you need for each project, but a basic knitting kit, like any tool kit, will be useful for many projects. Here is a list of helpers that will ease your knitting experience:

- Sets of knitting needles applicable to your project
- One or two crochet hooks for knitting repairs (sizes D, G, and H are enough for all projects here)
- Metal needle gauge with built-in, 6-inch ruler with holes for two knitting and crochet needle systems
- Small, retractable cloth or nylon tape measure with both centimeters and inches
- One large- and one medium-sized, blunt-pointed yarn needle
- Small, blunt-pointed scissors

Extras you may want to have:
- Plastic stitch markers (to mark an increase position on your needle)
- Stitch holder, similar to a blunt safety pin (for mittens, look for a 1–2" holder or use waste yarn)
- Egg-shaped darning egg and rounded ¾" dowel to support darning in ends (a dowel can also be used as a yarn ball winder)
- A nice knitting bag to hold your projects

Sizing: Thumbs Rule!

Even though the patterns in this book are arranged by named sizes (Men's medium, for instance), hand measurements and finished mitten measurements are given at the beginning of each pattern. The sizes are based on the theory that human body parts have fairly standard proportions: The girth of your wrist is half the girth of your neck, for instance; the length from fingertip to fingertip with arms outstretched is about the same as your height; your hand is as long as your face — that sort of thing.

With hands, it's the thumb that rules: The thumb is one-third the length of the hand. The thumb leaves the hand one-third of the way to the fingertips. Widthwise, the thumb is 40 percent as big around as the hand. However, the thumb itself is hard to measure. Not so the hand.

Place a ruler on a flat surface. Place your hand on top of it with the crease at the base of your palm at the zero line. Read the number at the tip of the middle finger. Divide that number by 3, and you get your thumb length. With that number and a calculator, you can figure all the length measurements of your hand.

To measure the circumference of your hand for a mitten, use a tape measure. Hold up your hand with the fingers touching and the thumb alongside the index finger. Measure around, just above the index finger knuckle, and include the tip of the thumb. That number is the girth of your mitten (or a loose glove) and allows just enough ease for comfort and proper insulation. Here's a formula for knitting a custom-fit mitten, if the hand you're knitting for falls between the given sizes:

> Hand length ÷ 3 = Thumb length
> Hand length + Thumb length = Finished mitten length, including cuff
> Hand circumference, including tip of thumb ÷ 2 = Finished mitten width
> Hand circumference, including tip of thumb x .40 = Mitten thumb circumference

When knitting for children, you might want to measure, then go up a size. Unlike their mittens, children never shrink!

Thumbies

Thumbs on mittens and gloves really do control the fit of a glove or mitten. In fact, thumbs are so important that, in some places, mittens are called "thumbies"! Dare to rip out a thumb that's too short, too narrow, too long, or too loose. Thumbs are quick to knit, and they are the soul of the mitten. If your thumb can't fully get into the mitten thumb, the rest of your hand won't be able to get in either. The total length of the thumb should be at least the amount given as the finished thumb length, or even a little longer (by about ¼–⅜"). If possible, try on the mitten before finishing the tips of the fingers and the thumb. The thumb crotch of the mitten should go all the way into the thumb crotch of the hand. "Pinch room" at the end of a wool mitten thumb quickly disappears in everyday shrinkage.

Be especially sure that the thumbs are correct on the two fulled mittens, as changes are nearly impossible to make once the mittens have been fulled.

Know-How to Do It

The most general instructions I can give you are to ask you to read the instructions and follow them. Whether you have knitted all your life or are just starting, many of the techniques here may be just a little different from those you have learned and can improve the appearance and wear of the mittens you make.

THE MAINE CAST-ON

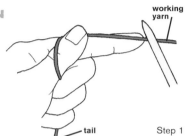

Step 1

The Maine cast-on gives a firm, slightly elastic edge and is the easiest cast-on to knit into that I've ever encountered. Plus, it keeps stockinette cuffs from curling at the edge. Follow these steps:

1. To cast on about 10 stitches, start about 18 inches from the end of the yarn, holding the end closest to the ball in your right hand and the short end in your left hand. Anchor both, ends downward, with your lesser fingers. Then, scoop your left thumb over, under, and up toward you, catching the yarn on the back of your thumb (this gives it a half twist).

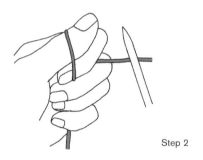

Step 2

2. Slide your index finger down into the loop, alongside your thumb, and transfer the loop to your index finger, pointing your finger away from you, like a pretend pistol (this gives it another half twist).

3. Insert the right needle into the loop knitwise, as if your index finger were the left needle. Use the long end of yarn to knit the loop off your finger onto the needle. Pull up firmly, first with your left hand, then with your right. Settle the stitch comfortably but firmly on the needle.

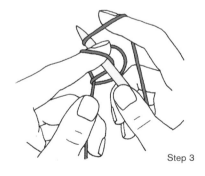

Step 3

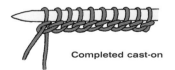

Completed cast-on

All but two of the patterns in the book are knit completely in the round on double-point needles. To knit in the round, divide the cast-on stitches among three needles evenly or as directed in the pattern. Form the needles into a triangle and use the fourth needle to join the triangle by knitting into the first stitch on the first needle. Take care that the cast-on stitches aren't twisted over the needles or between the needles when you make this join.

When you begin to knit, use the fourth needle to knit all the stitches on the first needle. Use the now-empty first needle to knit stitches on the second needle, and so forth. When you get to the end of the round, check to make sure all the stitches point downward and none are twisted over the needle, then *keep going.* Never turn around.

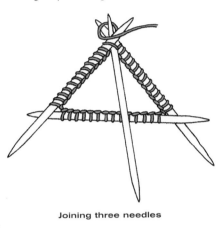

Joining three needles

Any Way You Splice It

There are various ways to join yarns of the same color in the middle of a project, but probably the oldest, best, and guaranteed most interesting (and disgusting) is the spit splice. Because saliva has a gluing effect on wool, it has been used for millennia by weavers and other fiber workers.

Pick apart about 1 inch of both the plies and the fibers in each ply until you have a fuzz of fibers at least a ½" long. Do this on both ends to be joined. Overlap these end to end. Next, lick or spit on the overlapped ends lavishly. Roll the overlaid ends together between your palms, hard and fast, so that you generate heat. Keep supplying spit and heat by rubbing until you have a strong join the same thickness as the yarn. Test to be sure the join holds by tugging gently.

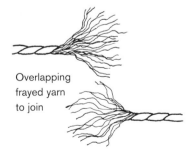

Overlapping frayed yarn to join

If you are knitting in more than one color, you will have to add on a second strand of yarn to your work. The directions will say, "Join contrast (or main) color."

About 7 stitches before you actually knit with it, start weaving in the new color. Hold the tail end pointing downward behind the next stitch, and knit around (or over) it, catching it in place. Then, knit under and over it for 6 stitches without knitting it at all, just as you would weave in a long float (see page 39). This will anchor the end firmly when you begin to knit.

To end a color, follow this method in reverse: After the last stitch with that color, break the yarn, leaving a 4-inch tail. Weave in the tail for the next 6 or 7 stitches. The patterns usually don't say to weave in the end, but do it anyway — it will save you time later!

If joining as above is completely inconvenient (for instance, if there are two colors to be joined at the same time), join the new color by sewing it into the back of the fabric with a yarn needle. Start where the color will begin, then darn the short end through the tops of purl stitches or floats on the inside of the mitten. Check to make sure it doesn't show on the outside.

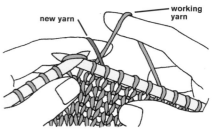

Knitting over new yarn

new yarn — working yarn

"Weaving in" shown on wrong side

When you finish the mitten, simply trim these woven-in ends. To avoid stretching the mitten by turning it inside out too often, wait until the mitten is finished to work in the cast-on tail, the tails at the base of the thumb, and the ends of the fingers and thumb.

Shape Up — and Out!

If hands had no thumbs, mittens would be straight, narrow, warm little bags. The thumb makes the hand suddenly wider where it begins at the wrist, then increasingly wider until the thumb separates from the hand, one-third of the way to the fingertips. Every mitten begins with the proposition that somehow there has to be room made for the thumb.

Many mittens have a series of increases on the thumb side just above the cuff. Some mittens have all the necessary stitches added immediately after the cuff. A few mittens start with fairly wide cuffs and are knitted straight to the narrowing at the end of the hand — the cuff is already wide enough to accommodate the thumb. The problem of the mitten falling off is sometimes taken care of with a little "waist" of ribbing knitted at the base of the hand.

Different shapings, traditions, and color patterns call for different methods of increasing to shape the thumb gore attractively. The increase most commonly used was invented by Elizabeth Zimmermann. Known as "make one" (M1), it's a little half-hitch thrown over the right needle either clockwise or counterclockwise to make it slant left or right. It is a nearly invisible increase with well-controlled tension, and it's easy to knit into in the next round.

You will encounter two other increases in this book. They are specific to knitting with two strands, as in color pattern work: knitting both strands into one stitch, and the two-for-one increase, which is used to make vertical stripes or ribs split apart into treelike formations.

Increases You'll Need for Mittens

- Make 1L and Make 1R for decorative lines at the thumb gore: See page 89.
- Knitting two colors into one stitch for Salt and Pepper pattern: See page 99.
- "Two-for-One Increase," for striped mittens: See page 73.

THUMBS UP!

One-third of the way up the hand, the thumb separates from the rest of the hand and there must be a hole in the mitten to accommodate that. For mittens with a thumb gore, there will be a gaping hole where you remove the gore stitches to continue up the hand. You'll need to cast on a specified number of stitches to bridge that gap. Here, I use the "twisted make one" (twisted M1) — a Maine cast-on method without the right-hand tail. It makes a nice firm edge that serves well when you come back to picking up the thumb stitches later in the process. **NOTE:** To keep the drawings that follow simple and thus clearer, they do not show the stitches already on the right-hand needle or the work below on the other side of the thumb hole.

1. Wrap the working yarn around your left thumb from front to back. Point your thumb upward.

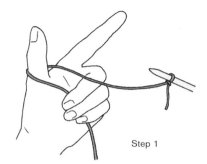

Step 1

2. Insert your left index finger down into the loop on your thumb and transfer the loop onto your index finger.

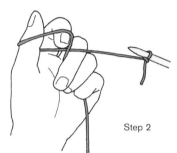

Step 2

3. Turn your index finger away from you, as if pointing a pretend pistol. Insert the right needle into the loop as if it were a stitch on a knitting needle. Slide the loop off your index finger and tighten it onto the right needle.

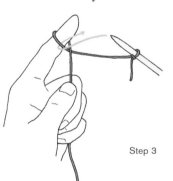

Step 3

Showing Your Colors

One color is nice, but two or more colors do things to each other, brightening or enhancing one another and changing a simple mitten into an accessory for outdoor wear. Three ways to add color to your mittens are to knit widthwise colored stripes, to knit large motifs on the back and simple patterns on the palm, or to knit repeating color patterns that wrap around the mitten. All of these color approaches use techniques that continue around the mitten, so you will have no bobbins, and you will never be knitting more than two strands at a time.

When two colors alternate over several rounds, patterns flower across the knitted fabric. Called jacquard, Fair Isle, stranding, color-work, or, locally in New England and Nova Scotia, "double knitting," its original function was to thicken the knit. For every little stitch with a hole in the middle, there is a strand of yarn behind it stopping the cold. The color patterns here are fairly simple but look difficult enough to enhance your reputation as a knitter.

The first axiom for color-work is: *Never twist the yarn.* The trick is to carry one color "ahead of" and below the other — in the direction of the knitting. This keeps the two yarns apart on the back of the work and the two strands won't twist, pull up irregularly, or get tangled. On the front, the color carried ahead (below the other) will dominate the color pattern consistently and smoothly. In extreme cases, like the striped pattern of Peek-a-Boo Mittens (page 70), carrying one color ahead causes it to stand up over the other color like the wales of corduroy.

If you move the yarn with your right forefinger, bring the dark color from under the other when you change colors; to change to the light color, lift it over the dark one.

**Bringing dark yarn
from underneath**

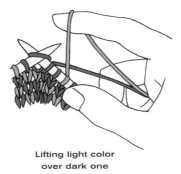

**Lifting light color
over dark one**

If you pick yarn from your left index finger, place the dark color to the left of the other on that finger. Never dig under one color to get at the other.

If you knit with both hands, hold the main (or dark) color on the left forefinger and the contrasting (or light) color on the right, pick from the left and "throw" the right. This "stranding" is associated with Norwegian knitting.

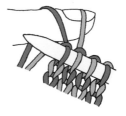

**Using left-hand
technique**

Stop-and-Go Mittens

Mittens don't have to be identical, use brand new, expensive yarn, or take a long time to make. They can have a similar theme, use small amounts of left-over yarn, and be super quick. The mittens pictured were made of purchased blue yarn and small amounts of Kool-Aid-dyed white yarn (see list below); you may use any yarn that will provide the required gauge. Simply constructed, with stripes as an easily visible measure, Stop-and-Go Mittens knit up quickly and are practical for kids — they can be worn on either hand.

Sizes
Child's 2–3 years, 4–6 years, 6–8 years

Yarn
Rauma Vamsegarn 3-ply, bulky
    weight, 100% wool
mc: 1 skein royal blue (#V67)
all ccs: 1 skein white (#V00)

Needles
One set #2 (2.75mm) dp needles, for
    ribbing

One set #3 (3.25mm) dp needles, *or
    size you need to knit correct gauge*

Gauge
5 sts = 1" (2.5cm) on larger needles
    in St st

Other supplies
Stitch marker, 12" (30cm) waste
    yarn, yarn needle

---

cc = contrast color ◆ **dp** = double point ◆ **K** = knit ◆ **K2tog** = knit 2 together ◆ **M1** = make 1 ◆ **mc** = main color ◆ **P** = purl ◆ **rnd(s)** = round(s) ◆ **st(s)** = stitch(es) ◆ **St st** = stockinette stitch

SIZES	2–3 YRS	4–6 YRS	6–8 YRS
Hand length	4½"	5½"	6"
Thumb length	1½"	1¾"	2" .
Hand circumference, including thumb tip	5"	6"	7"
Finished mitten length	6"	7⅓"	8"
Finished thumb length	1½"	1¾"	2"
Finished mitten width	2½"	3"	3½"
RIBBING THE CUFF			
Choose a stripe pattern from the charts on page 20. With smaller needles and mc (first color of stripe pattern), cast on	27 sts	30 sts	36 sts

Distribute stitches on three dp needles:
    On Needle 1:
    On Needle 2:
    On Needle 3:
	9 sts
	9 sts
	9 sts
		12 sts
		9 sts
		9 sts
			12 sts
			12 sts
			12 sts

Join in rnd, being careful not to twist sts.			
With mc, *K2, P1; repeat from * to end of rnd.			
Count previous rnd as first rnd of stripe pattern. Following the stripe pattern, work K2, P1 ribbing until cuff measures	1½"	1¾"	2"
NOTE: When you get to the last stripe of the cuff, complete it if it adds only a rnd or two over the suggested cuff length.			
STARTING THE HAND AND THUMB GORE			
Rounds 1–4: Change to larger needles and St st. Maintaining stripe pattern, knit to end of rnd.			
Round 5: K1, M1L, K1, M1R, place marker, knit to end of rnd. The 3 sts *between* the first st and the marker are the beginning of the thumb gore. On Needle 1 you will have	11 sts	14 sts	14 sts

	2–3 YRS	4–6 YRS	6–8 YRS
Round 6: Knit to end of rnd.			
Round 7: K1, M1L, knit to marker, M1R (slip marker), knit to end of rnd.			
Repeat Rounds 6 and 7	0 more times	1 more time	2 more times
Between the first st and the marker you will have	5 sts	7 sts	9 sts
Knit even in stripe pattern until the thumb gore has the same number of stripes as the cuff, or until the gore measures	1½"	1¾"	2"
MAKING THE THUMB HOLE			
Next Round: K1, place on a piece of waste yarn	5 sts	7 sts	9 sts
With twisted M1 (page 14), cast on 4 sts over the thumb hole. You will have	30 sts	33 sts	39 sts
Working in striped pattern, knit until mitten is finished length (page 18), less	6 rnds	6 rnds	8 rnds
DECREASING THE MITTEN TIP			
Distribute sts evenly on three dp needles: On Needle 1: On Needle 2: On Needle 3:	10 sts 10 sts 10 sts	11 sts 11 sts 11 sts	13 sts 13 sts 13 sts
Round 1: Working in stripe pattern, K2tog at both ends of all needles.			
Round 2: Knit even to end of rnd.			
Repeat Rounds 1 and 2	2 more times	2 more times	3 more times
You will have	12 sts	15 sts	15 sts
Break yarn. Using yarn needle, thread yarn end through remaining sts. Draw yarn end through sts one more time. Pull firmly to close, and draw yarn end to inside of mitten.			

KNITTING THE THUMB	2–3 YRS	4–6 YRS	6–8 YRS
Next Round: From waste yarn, pick up	5 sts	7 sts	9 sts
Pick up 4 sts from top of thumb hole. In each corner, pick up one side of a st, twisting it as you place it on the needle. You will have	11 sts	13 sts	15 sts
Working in stripe pattern, knit until length from end of cuff measures	2¾"	3¼"	3¾"
DECREASING THUMB TIP			
Round 1: *K1, K2tog; repeat from * to end of rnd, knitting the last	2 sts	1 st	0 sts
Round 2: Knit to end of rnd.			
Repeat Rounds 1 and 2	0 times	1 time	1 time
You will have	8 sts	6 sts	7 sts
Break yarn. Using yarn needle, thread yarn end through remaining sts. Draw yarn end through sts one more time. Pull firmly to close, and draw end to inside of mitten.			
FINISHING			
Turn mitten inside out, darn yarn ends into fabric, and trim close to fabric. Make second mitten.			

STRIPING PATTERN CHARTS

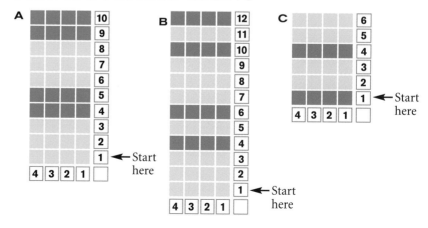

Colors from the Kitchen

Kool-Aid dyeing is fun and fast. Use colors straight from the package, or experiment by mixing "flavors"! You can get quite intense colors by increasing the amount of powder for each ½ cup of water you use. Purchase packages of unsweetened Kool-Aid in several flavors. You'll want to experiment to discover what colors the various flavors and combinations of flavors produce.

1. Wind off approximately 5-yard lengths of white or unbleached yarn. (I used wool, but you can experiment with other fibers, including synthetics, as well.) Wrap the lengths around your hand to make small skeins. Use the yarn ends to tie the skeins *very loosely* around the middle.

2. Soak the skeins in an 8:1 solution of water and white vinegar while you prepare the Kool-Aid dye baths.

3. Pour about ⅓ to ½ cup of hot water into an 8-ounce, microwave-safe glass or a paper cup. Add a package of Kool-Aid to the water and stir to mix thoroughly.

4. Squeeze the vinegar-water from a skein of yarn and place the skein in the dyebath mixture. Submerse the skein completely and stir gently to ensure that the dye mixture thoroughly saturates the fibers.

5. Place the glass in your microwave (you can do several glassfuls at once). Microwave on HIGH for 2 minutes. Stir gently and let rest for 2 minutes. Microwave on HIGH for 2 more minutes.

6. Allow the yarn to cool in the glass, or pour it into a strainer and allow it to air-dry. Do not try to cool the hot yarn by rinsing it under cold water, as this may cause the fibers to begin to felt.

7. When the yarn is cool enough to handle, rinse it with water that is about the same temperature as the yarn. Rinse until no more color comes out of the yarn. Allow the yarn to air-dry, then it's ready to use. To speed the drying process, spin the yarn in your washer for a few minutes, or roll it in a towel to absorb some of the water before hanging it to dry.

Polar Bear Mitts

Based on a mitten from northern Sweden, the Polar Bear Mitt, worn alone or over lightweight mittens, is the ultimate thick, soft mitten. Some of the measurements may seem large, but after shrinking, the mitts will settle down to the size you knitted. The mitten pictured was knit with the yarn listed below; you may use any yarn that will provide the required gauge.

Sizes

Women's small, Women's medium,
    Men's medium

Yarn

Peace Fleece 2-ply, worsted weight,
    30% mohair/70% wool
mc: 2 skeins Antarctic White
cc A, B, and C: 1½ yds (1.35m) each
    color Persian embroidery yarn

Needles

One set #10½ (6.5mm) dp needles,
    or size you need to knit correct gauge

Gauge

3 sts = 1"/2.5cm in St st (shrinks to
    3½ sts = 1"/2.5cm after fulling)

Other supplies

12" (30cm) waste yarn, yarn needle,
    two dishpans, shampoo or
    Murphy's Oil Soap, washboard
    or felting board, fine wire brush
    or pet comb (pet slicker)

---

cc = contrast color ◆ **K** = knit
K2tog = knit 2 together
M1 = make one ◆ **mc** = main
color ◆ **rnd(s)** = round(s)
ssk2tog = slip, slip, knit 2
together ◆ **st(s)** = stitch(es)
St st = stockinette stitch

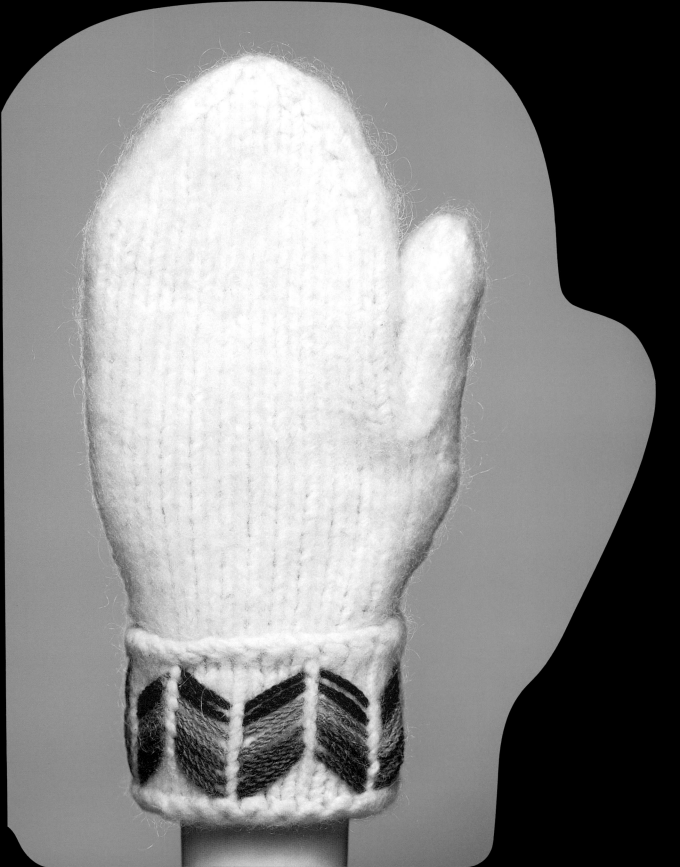

SIZES	WOMEN'S S	WOMEN'S M	MEN'S M
Hand length	6¾"	7½"	7½"
Thumb length	2¼"	2½"	2½"
Hand circumference, including thumb tip	8"	9"	10"
Pre-fulled mitten length (cuff extended)	12"	14¾"	14¾"
Pre-fulled thumb length	2¾"	3½"	3½"
Pre-fulled mitten width	4½"	4¾"	5¼"
Fulled mitten length, cuff turned up	9"	9¾"	9¾"
Fulled mitten thumb length	2½"	3"	3"
Fulled mitten width	4"	4½"	5"
MAKING THE CUFF AND WRIST			
Cast on	28 sts	32 sts	35 sts
Distribute sts evenly on three dp needles. Join in rnd; don't twist sts. Knit even for	2¼"	2½"	2½"
Turn work inside out, and knit to end of rnd. (Your first st will be into the st you just knitted, and the "purl" sts of the cuff will face you.)			
Knit even until length from the cast-on edge measures	6¾"	8½"	8½"
MAKING THE THUMB HOLE (Right Mitten)			
Next Round: Knit 1. Place on a piece of waste yarn	4 sts	5 sts	5 sts
With twisted M1 (page 14), cast on	4 sts	5 sts	5 sts
Knit to end of rnd. You will have	28 sts	32 sts	35 sts
MAKING THE THUMB HOLE (Left Mitten)			
Round 1: Knit to last	5 sts	6 sts	6 sts
Slip on holder the next	4 sts	5 sts	5 sts

	WOMEN'S S	WOMEN'S M	MEN'S M
Knit 1. With twisted M1 (page 14), cast on	4 sts	5 sts	5 sts
You will have	28 sts	32 sts	35 sts
KNITTING THE HAND			
Knit even until length above thumb hole measures	3"	3¾"	3¾"
DECREASING THE MITTEN TIP			
Distribute sts on three dp needles: On Needle 1: On Needle 2: On Needle 3:	14 sts 7 sts 7 sts	16 sts 8 sts 8 sts	18 sts 9 sts 8 sts
Round 1 Needle 1: K1, ssk2tog, knit to last 3 sts, K2tog, K1. Needle 2: K1, ssk2tog, knit to end of needle. Needle 3: Knit to last 3 sts on needle, K2tog, K1.			
You will have	24 sts	28 sts	31 sts
Rounds 2 and 3: Knit to end of rnd.			
Repeat Rounds 1–3	3 more times	4 more times	5 more times
You will have	12 sts	12 sts	11 sts
Break yarn, leaving a 6–8" tail. With yarn needle, draw up remaining sts on tail. Thread the tail through the sts again, and pull firmly to close. Draw tail inside mitten.			
KNITTING THE THUMB			
Pick up from the waste yarn	4 sts	5 sts	5 sts
Pick up from the cast-on sts at the top of the hole	4 sts	5 sts	5 sts
Pick up the sides of corner sts, twisting them onto the needle. Take from each corner	1 st	1 st	1, 2 sts

Topping It Off

The tips of mittens narrow from a hand's width to almost nothing. Some tips are pointed like housetops, some are bordered with decorative "decrease bands," and others are rounded. Almost all use the same two methods of decreasing, but in different arrangements.

Slip, slip, knit two together (ssk2tog). Slip two stitches, one at a time, from your left needle to your right, as if to knit. Then insert the left needle from left to right through the front loops of the slipped stitches and knit the two stitches together from this position. This technique makes a stitch that slants left.

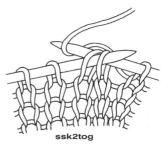

ssk2tog

Knit two together (K2tog). Knit two stitches together by inserting the needle knitwise into both loops, as you would to knit a single stitch. The stitch it creates slants right.

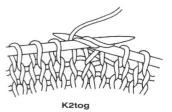

K2tog

	WOMEN'S S	WOMEN'S M	MEN'S M
You will have	10 sts	12 sts	14 sts
Distribute sts on three dp needles:			
On Needle 1:	4 sts	4 sts	5 sts
On Needle 2:	3 sts	4 sts	5 sts
On Needle 3:	3 sts	4 sts	4 sts
Knit in rnds until length from start of thumb measures	2¼"	2½"	3½"
DECREASING THE THUMB TIP			
Round 1: Ssk2tog at beginning of each needle and then knit to end of needle. You will have	7 sts	9 sts	11 sts
Round 2: Knit to end of rnd.			

	WOMEN'S S	WOMEN'S M	MEN'S M
Repeat Rounds 1 and 2	0 more times	1 more time	2 more times
You will have	7 sts	6 sts	5 sts
Next Round: Knit to end of rnd.			
Break yarn, leaving a 6–8" tail. With yarn needle, draw up remaining sts on tail. Thread the tail through the sts again, and pull firmly to close. Draw tail inside mitten.			
FINISHING			
Turn mitten inside out and darn yarn ends on wrong side of mitten.			
Shrink and full the mittens following the directions on page 51.			
When completely dry after fulling, apply embroidery in brightly colored worsted-weight wool or tripled wool embroidery yarn, following chart below.			

Embroidered Cuff

The counted-stitch embroidery for the Polar Bear Mitts is borrowed from an old style used on needle-netted mittens in northern Sweden before the invention of knitting.

Follow the pattern at right in the colors of your choice, counting rows up and down, half stitches right and left. For counted-stitch embroidery, use a blunt yarn needle and stitch through loops of knitted stitches.

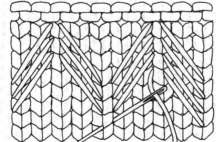

Lillemor's Mittens

My mother-in-law, Lillemor Orm Hansen, knitted many of these simple, cozy mittens for our family. To make these mittens you never purl. The mitten and cuff are a flat square of garter stitch, stitched lengthwise to form a tube. The thumb and fingertips are picked up and knitted in the round. Garter stitch is thick, even surfaced, and elastic, ideal clothing for growing people. The mitten pictured was knit with yarn listed below; you may use any yarn that will provide the required gauge.

Sizes

Adult's small, medium, large

Yarn

Brown Sheep Lamb's Pride, worsted
weight, 85% wool/15% mohair

mc: 1 skein Butterfly Blue

cc: 1 skein Peruvian Pink

Needles

One set #4 (3.5mm) dp needles, *or
size you need to knit correct gauge*

Optionally, a pair of straight needles,
#4 (3.5mm), *for garter stitch
portion*

Gauge

5½ sts = 1" (2.5cm) in garter stitch

Other supplies

42" (106.75cm) third color waste
yarn, yarn needle

---

cc = contrast color ◆ **dp** =
double point ◆ **K** = knit
K2tog = knit 2 together
mc = main color ◆ **rnd(s)** =
round(s) ◆ **rs** = right side
ssk2tog = slip, slip, knit 2
together ◆ **st(s)** = stitches

SIZES	SMALL	MEDIUM	LARGE
Hand length	6"	7½"	9"
Thumb length	2"	2½"	3"
Finished mitten length	8"	10"	12"
Finished thumb length	2"	2½"	3"
Finished mitten width	3"	4"	5"
KNITTING THE GARTER STITCH SQUARE			
With mc, cast on	34 sts	44 sts	56 sts
Rows 1–6: With two needles and mc, knit throughout, turning work at end of rows. Consider the rs as the one with the cast-on tail at the right (odd-numbered rows).			
Rows 7 and 8: With cc, knit. Carry yarn not in use at end of rows.			
Rows 9–12: With mc, knit.			
Repeat Rows 7–12 in garter stitch until work length measures	4"	5"	6"

Tips and Tricks with Garter Stitch

- To work the garter stitch square, knit on both the right and the wrong sides of the piece, turning at the end of each row.
- To make a one-row stripe in garter stitch, start on the right side and knit two rows with the contrast color. After the next row of another color, the second color will show as two dotted lines on the wrong side of the work.
- To count garter stitch rows, count purl ridges on the right side and multiply by 2. To count stitches across a row, count the top (bump) of each purl stitch.
- To measure the length of garter stitch fabric, do not stretch the fabric.

MAKING THE THUMB HOLE (Right Mitten)	SMALL	MEDIUM	LARGE
Finish the next wrong side row.			
Next row: With mc, knit	17 sts	22 sts	28 sts
With 18" of waste yarn, knit	7 sts	9 sts	11 sts
Slip the waste yarn sts just knit back onto left needle, and with working yarn, knit the waste yarn sts again. Knit to end of row. (Stitches worked in waste yarn will later be used for the thumb hole. For illustration, see page 45.) You will have	34 sts	44 sts	56 sts
MAKING THE THUMB HOLE (Left Mitten)			
Finish the next rs row.			
Next Row: With mc, knit	17 sts	22 sts	28 sts
With 12" of waste yarn, knit	7 sts	9 sts	11 sts
Slip waste yarn sts just knit back onto left needle; with working yarn, knit waste yarn sts again. Knit to end of row. You will have	34 sts	44 sts	56 sts
CONTINUING THE HAND			
Continue knitting back and forth in rows in stripe pattern until work measures	6"	8"	10"
Finish the next wrong side row. Thread all sts onto 12" length of waste yarn. Don't break working yarn.			
SEWING UP THE HAND			
Fold the garter stitch square with rs facing and the lengthwise edges together. With mc on yarn needle, sew the lengthwise edges together. Turn rs out.			
DECREASING THE MITTEN TIP			
With rs out, distribute sts on three dp needles: On Needle 1: On Needle 2: On Needle 3:	17 sts 9 sts 8 sts	22 sts 11 sts 11 sts	28 sts 14 sts 14 sts

	SMALL	MEDIUM	LARGE
Rounds 1–5: Using a fourth needle, knit the stitches on Needle 1. When that needle is empty, use it to knit Needle 2, and so forth. *Never turn back.*			
NOTE: In the following rnds, you decrease at both ends of Needle 1, at the beginning of Needle 2, and at the end of Needle 3.			
Round 6 Needle 1: K1, K2tog, knit to last 2 sts on needle, ssk2tog. Needle 2: K1, K2tog, knit to end of needle. Needle 3: Knit to last 2 sts on needle, ssk2tog. You will have	30 sts	40 sts	52 sts
Repeat Round 6 until 12 sts remain.			
Break yarn, leaving a 6–8" tail. With yarn needle, draw remaining sts up on tail. Thread tail through sts again and pull firmly to close. Draw tail inside mitten.			
KNITTING THE THUMB			
Working on the rs, carefully remove the waste yarn at the thumb hole, slipping open sts onto two dp needles, one needle for the lower edge and one needle for the upper edge.			
Along the lower edge you will have	7 sts	9 sts	11 sts
Along the upper edge you will have	6 sts	8 sts	10 sts
With rs out, distribute sts on three dp needles: On Needle 1: On Needle 2: On Needle 3:	6 sts 3 sts 4 sts	8 sts 5 sts 4 sts	10 sts 6 sts 5 sts
Pick up 1 st in each corner by taking half of a stitch and giving it a twist as you place it on the needle. Place 1 st on each end of Needle 1. You will have	15 sts	19 sts	23 sts

	SMALL	MEDIUM	LARGE
Round 1: With mc, knit to end of rnd.			
Round 2 Needle 1: Ssk2tog, knit to 2 sts before end of needle, K2tog. Needles 2 and 3: Knit to end of rnd. You will have	13 sts	17 sts	21 sts
Knit even in rnds until thumb length is	1½"	2"	2½"
DECREASING THE THUMB TIP			
Round 1: Ssk2tog the first 2 sts of each needle, then knit to end of needle. You will have	10 sts	14 sts	18 sts
Repeat Round 1 until there remain	4 sts	6 sts	6 sts
Break yarn, leaving a 6–8" tail. With yarn needle, draw up remaining sts on the tail. Thread the tail through the sts again, and pull up firmly to close. Draw tail inside mitten.			
FINISHING			
Turn mitten inside out and darn all ends into back of fabric.			

The Inside Story

Your knitting will go faster and you will be less stressed if you pull the yarn from the center of the ball instead of unwinding it from the outside. Many yarns come in so-called "pull skeins," which can be pulled from the center. Other yarns come as hanks that must be wound into balls. Your yarn shop may wind skeins for you on a ball winder. Or wind your yarn on a short stick or your thumb. Hold the starting end aside as you wind so that you can pull the yarn from inside when you knit.

Chicky Feet Mittens

This is the most charming pattern I've seen. As a baby pattern, it's perfect. I'd like to use it someday in a sweater design with little partridge chicks across the shoulders. Remember to catch the contrast color strand on the long floats in the middle of each set of feet, or little fingers will get caught! The mittens pictured were knit with yarn listed below; you may use any yarn that will provide the required gauge.

Sizes

Child's 1 year, 2 years, 4 years

Yarn

Rauma Babygarn, fingering weight,
    100% merino wool
mc: 1 skein red (#B18)
cc: 1 skein orange (#B60)

Needles

One set #1 (2.25mm) dp needles, for
    ribbing
One set #2 (2.75mm) dp needles, *or
    size you need to knit correct gauge*

Gauge

9 sts = 1" (2.5cm) on larger needles in
    Chicky Feet pattern

Other supplies

Stitch holder, yarn needle

---

beg = beginning ◆ **cc** =
contrast color ◆ **cont** =
continue ◆ **dp** = double point
inc = increase/increasing
K = knit ◆ **K2tog** = knit 2
together ◆ **mc** = main color
P = purl ◆ **rnd(s)** = round(s)
st(s) = stitch(es)

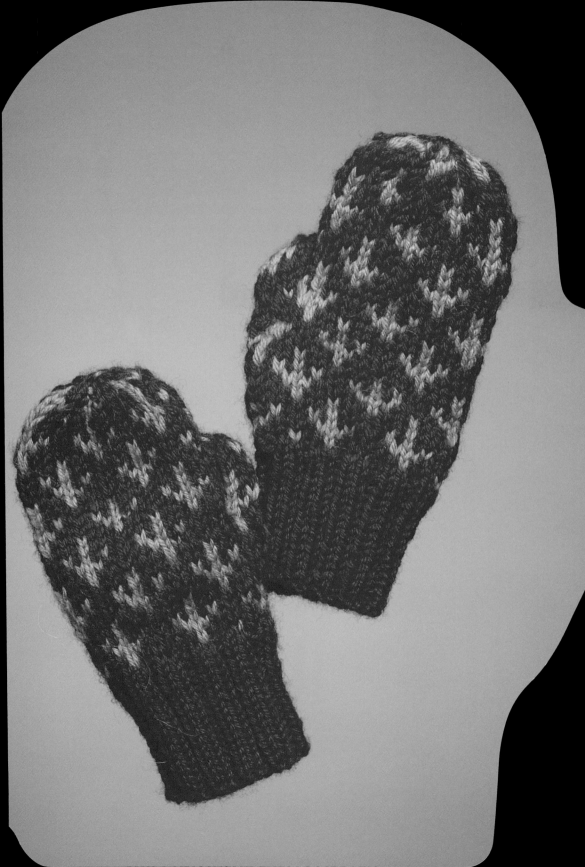

SIZES	1 YR	2 YRS	4 YRS
Hand length	3⅜"	3¾"	4½"
Thumb length	1⅛"	1¼"	1½"
Finished mitten length	4½"	5¼"	6¼"
Finished mitten width	2⅛"	3⅛"	3½"
MAKING THE CUFF			
With mc and smaller needles, cast on	40 sts	48 sts	56 sts
Distribute sts evenly on three dp needles. Join rnd, being careful not to twist the sts.			
Round 1: *K2, P2; repeat from * to end rnd.			
Repeat Round 1 for	1½"	1¾"	2¼"
KNITTING THE PATTERN AND THUMB GORE			
NOTE: Left and right mittens are identical.			
Round 1: With larger needles, work Line 1 of Thumb Gore chart (page 39), reading from right to left, then move to Line 1 of Chicky Feet chart and knit right to left. Repeat pattern chart until end of rnd. Carry cc ahead at all times (pages 14–15).			
Round 2: Work Line 2 of both charts.			
Round 3: Work Line 3 of both charts, inc as indicated on Thumb Gore chart by M1R, K1 (center st), M1L (page 89).			
Cont to knit across Thumb Gore chart at beginning of every rnd, increasing in Rounds 5, 7, and 9 as shown on Thumb Gore chart, and cont with Chicky Feet chart to end of each rnd.			
When all increases are completed (four inc rnds in all), you will have	48 sts	56 sts	64 sts
Work two rnds in pattern on all sts, ending with Line 11 on Thumb Gore chart.			

CONTINUING THE HAND	1 YR	2 YRS	4 YRS
Next Round: Knit	3 sts	2 sts	1 st
Place on stitch holder the next	11 sts	13 sts	15 sts
With twisted M1 (page 14), cast on over gap	3 sts	5 sts	7 sts
You will have	40 sts	48 sts	56 sts
Knit even until hand (above cuff) is	2¾"	3¼"	3¾"
Stop after completing Line 4 or Line 8 of Chicky Feet pattern.			
DECREASING AFTER LINE 4			
If you ended with Line 4 of pattern, follow these instructions:			
Round 1: K1 cc, *K1 mc, K2tog mc, K1 cc; repeat from * to end of rnd.			
Round 2: *K2tog mc, K3 cc, K1 mc; repeat from * to end of rnd.			
Round 3: *K2tog mc, K1 cc, K2tog mc; repeat from * to end of rnd. You will have	15 sts	18 sts	21 sts
Break cc yarn; pull yarn end inside mitten. Go to "Completing Mitten Tip" on page 38.			
DECREASING AFTER LINE 8			
If you ended with Line 8 of pattern, follow these instructions:			
Round 1: K1 mc, *K1 mc, K2tog mc, K1 cc; repeat from * to end of rnd.			
Round 2: K1 cc, *K1 cc, K2tog mc, K1 mc, K2 cc; repeat from * to end of rnd.			
Round 3: K2tog mc, *K1 cc, [K2tog mc] twice; repeat from * to end of rnd. You will have	15 sts	18 sts	21 sts
Break cc yarn; pull yarn end inside mitten. Go to "Completing Mitten Tip" on page 38.			

COMPLETING MITTEN TIP	1 YR	2 YRS	4 YRS
Next Round: *K1, K2tog; repeat from * to end of rnd. You will have	10 sts	12 sts	14 sts
Break mc yarn, leaving a 6–8" tail. Using yarn needle, thread end through sts on needle. Pull firmly to close; pull end inside mitten.			
KNITTING THE THUMB			
With three smaller dp needles, pick up from stitch holder	11 sts	13 sts	15 sts
Pick up from cast-on edge of thumb hole	3 sts	5 sts	7 sts
Pick up 2 sts in each corner, twisting them as you place them on needle. You will have	18 sts	22 sts	26 sts
Distribute sts evenly on three needles, keeping beg of rnd at beg of thumb gore.			
Join both yarns. Knit in pattern to right corner of thumb gore, K2tog. **NOTE:** Pattern doesn't come out even in size 2 years; in this size only, knit first 4 sts of Chicky Feet chart on these 4 sts for entire length of thumb.			
You will have	16 sts	20 sts	24 sts
Knit even until thumb measures	¾"	1"	1¼"
Next Round: *K1, K2tog; repeat from * to end of rnd, matching colors as best you can.			
Knit one rnd even.			
Next Round: *K1, K2tog; repeat from * to end of rnd.			
Break yarn, leaving a 6–8" tail. Using yarn needle, thread end through sts on needle. Draw end through sts once more as you remove them from the needles. Pull firmly to close; draw yarn end inside mitten.			
FINISHING			
Darn all loose ends inside mitten. Trim close to fabric. Make second mitten same as first.			

Chicky Feet Patterns

Gaps in Thumb Gore chart show increase sites. Knit across gaps as if they don't exist. Increase on *both* sides of the center stitch, as shown.

THUMB GORE

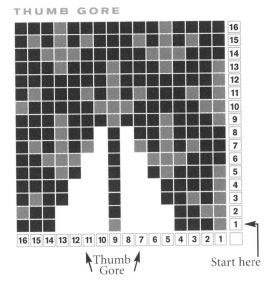

CHICKY FEET

Thumb Gore

Start here

Anchor Your Floats

When you knit two colors in a pattern, one strand always lies behind each stitch. When there are four or more stitches of the same color in a row, there will be a long strand, or float, of the second color attached only at the ends. This can catch on your jewelry or fingernails, and if a float pulls or breaks, it will make a hole in your mitten or pull the design out of shape. "Weaving in" is the solution. Here's how:

Right-hand knitting: Give the two yarns a half twist before the third stitch and a half twist back before the fourth stitch of the single color run.

Left-hand knitting: Duck in under the strand you want to weave with the needle tip and knit the other strand from there. Knit the next stitch as usual, from above both strands.

Two-hand knitting (stranding): Lift the left-hand strand over the needle tips while you knit under it. Drop it to its usual place and continue knitting over it as before. This weaves it in between both stitches. To weave in the right-hand strand, insert the needle in the next stitch, bring the right strand under the right needle and hold it to the left of (but over) the left strand while you knit the left strand as usual. Bring the right strand back where it belongs and knit the next stitch as usual.

Fleur-de-Lis Mittens

With its simple pattern and almost no shaping, this mitten is a good first color-knitting project. The tip and thumb are knitted in one color, and there is no thumb gore. Some rounds seem to have three colors, but only two are used at a time. The mitten pictured was knit with yarn listed below; you may use any yarn that will provide the required gauge. Add stripes to the cuff or leave it plain, as per the directions.

Sizes
Child's 8–10 years, Women's small, Women's medium

Yarn
Brown Sheep Lamb's Pride, worsted weight, 85% wool/15% mohair
mc: 1 skein Blue Heirloom
cc A: 1 skein Aztec Turquoise
cc B: 1 skein Brite Blue
cc C: 1 skein Emerald Fantasy

Needles
One set #2 (2.75mm) dp needles, for ribbing
One set #3 (3.25mm) dp needles, *or size you need to knit correct gauge*

Gauge
7 sts = 1" (2.5cm) on larger needles in Fleur-de-Lis pattern

Other supplies
24" (61cm) cc waste yarn, yarn needle

---

cc = contrast color ◆ **dp** = double point ◆ **K** = knit ◆ **K2tog** = knit 2 together ◆ **mc** = main color ◆ **P** = purl **rnd(s)** = round(s) **ssk2tog** = slip, slip, knit 2 together ◆ **st(s)** = stitch(es)

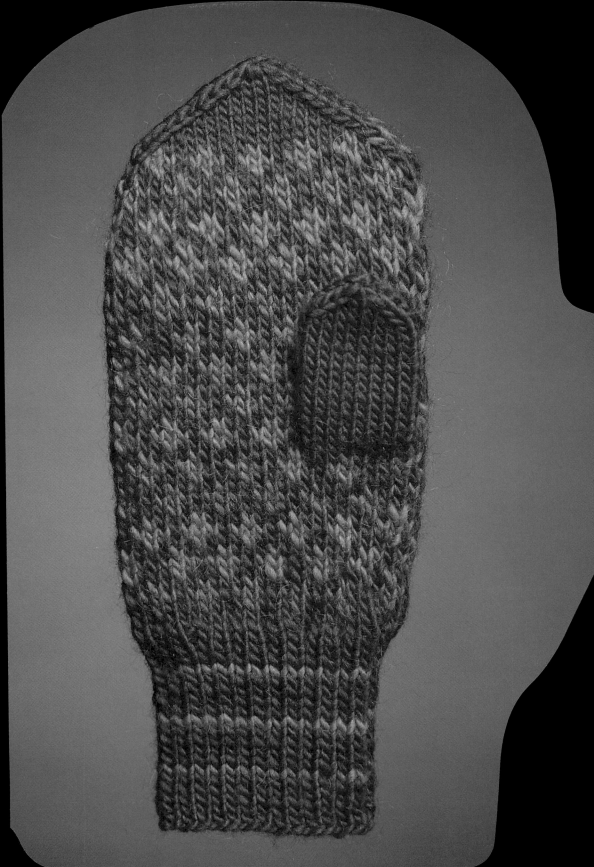

SIZE	8–10 YRS	WOMEN'S S	WOMEN'S M
Hand length	6½"	7"	7½"
Thumb length	2⅙"	2⅓"	2½"
Hand circumference above knuckles, including tip of thumb	8"	8¼"	9"
Finished mitten length	8¾"	9⅓"	10"
Finished thumb length	2¼"	2⅓"	2½"
Finished mitten width	4"	4¼"	4½"
MAKING THE CUFF			
On smaller needles, cast on	45 sts	48 sts	51 sts

Distribute sts on three dp needles:
    On Needle 1:
    On Needle 2:
    On Needle 3:
	
	15 sts
	15 sts
	15 sts
		
		18 sts
		15 sts
		15 sts
			
			18 sts
			18 sts
			15 sts

Join in rnd, being careful not to twist sts.			
Round 1: *K2, P1; repeat from * to end rnd.			
Continue working K2, P1 ribbing in rnds until length from cast-on edge measures	2¼"	2⅓"	2½"
STARTING THE HAND			

Inc by M1 between knit sts of ribbing:
    Needle 1:
    Needle 2:
    Needle 3:
	
	3 times
	2 times
	2 times
		
		3 times
		3 times
		2 times
			
			3 times
			3 times
			3 times

You will have	52 sts	56 sts	60 sts
STARTING THE PATTERN			
Begin Fleur-de-Lis pattern, following chart (page 45). Read each line from right to left, starting with Line 1 at bottom. Repeat 4-st pattern until length above cuff measures	2¼"	2⅓"	2½"
End after completing Line 3, 6, or 9.			
MAKING THE THUMB HOLE *(Right Mitten)*			
Next Round: K1, then with 12" length of cc waste yarn, knit	8 sts	8 sts	9 sts

	8–10 YRS	WOMEN'S S	WOMEN'S M
Place the 8 sts just knit in waste yarn back on left needle (see illustration, page 45).			
Re-knit waste yarn sts in pattern. Knit in pattern to end of rnd. (Sts in waste yarn will later be picked out to create thumb opening. Don't weave in waste yarn ends.)			
MAKING THE THUMB HOLE *(Left Mitten)*			
Next Round: Knit in pattern to last	9 sts	9 sts	10 sts
With 12" length of cc waste yarn, knit	8 sts	8 sts	9 sts
Place the 8 sts just knit in waste yarn back on left needle (see illustration, page 45).			
Re-knit waste-yarn sts in pattern. K1 in pattern to complete rnd.			
CONTINUING THE HAND			
Knit even in pattern until length above cuff measures	4½"	5"	5½"
DECREASING THE MITTEN TIP			

Without moving the beginning or end of rnd, redistribute the sts on the needles:
    On Needle 1:
    On Needle 2:
    On Needle 3:
	26 sts
	13 sts
	13 sts
		28 sts
		14 sts
		14 sts
			30 sts
			15 sts
			15 sts

Round 1 Needle 1: Knit in pattern to 2 sts before end of needle (little finger side), K2tog. Needle 2: Ssk2tog; knit in pattern to end of needle. Needle 3: Knit in pattern to end of needle.			
Round 2: Knit even in pattern.			
Rounds 3 and 4: Repeat Rounds 1 and 2. You will have	48 sts	52 sts	56 sts

	8–10 YRS	WOMEN'S S	WOMEN'S M
Round 5 Needle 1: Ssk2tog, knit to 2 sts before end of needle, K2tog. Needle 2: Ssk2tog, knit to end of needle. Needle 3: Knit to 2 sts before end of needle, K2tog.			
Round 6: Knit even in pattern.			
Rounds 7 and 8: Repeat Rounds 5 and 6.			
You will have	40 sts	44 sts	48 sts
Break cc yarn, and draw yarn end to inside. Continue in mc only, repeating Round 5 until there are	12 sts	12 sts	12 sts
Break yarn. With yarn needle, draw remaining sts up on yarn end. Thread yarn through sts again and pull firmly closed.			
KNITTING THE THUMB			
Carefully pick out waste yarn at thumb hole, slipping open sts onto two dp needles (one needle for the lower edge and one needle for the upper edge).			
Add 1 st at each end of the top needle sts by picking up one more partly open bottom loop on each side. On the top edge you will have	9 sts	9 sts	10 sts
At each corner, pick up the side of a st and twist it as you place it on the bottom needle. You will have	10 sts	10 sts	11 sts

Distribute sts on three dp needles, with Needle 1 at the top of the thumb hole:
    On Needle 1:
    On Needle 2:
    On Needle 3:
	9 sts
	5 sts
	5 sts
		9 sts
		5 sts
		5 sts
			10 sts
			5 sts
			6 sts

Starting with Needle 1, with mc only, K2, K2tog, knit to end of rnd. You will have	18 sts	18 sts	20 sts

	8–10 YRS	WOMEN'S S	WOMEN'S M
Knit even in mc only until thumb measures	2"	2"	2¼"
DECREASING THE THUMB TIP			
Repeat Rounds 5–6 of "Decreasing the Mitten Tip" (page 43) until you have	6 sts	6 sts	8 sts
Break yarn. With yarn needle, draw up remaining sts on tail. Thread yarn end through sts again and pull firmly to close. Draw end to inside of mitten.			
FINISHING			
Turn mitten inside out and darn in all loose ends. Trim close to fabric. Make a second mitten.			

FLEUR-DE-LIS CHART

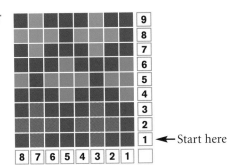

← Start here

Knitting on Waste Yarn

On mittens where there are an equal number of stitches above and below the thumb hole, you can knit with a piece of waste yarn for the specified number of stitches, then backtrack, placing the stitches just knit back on the left-hand needle. Next, knit the waste yarn stitches with the working yarn, in pattern, and continue on. Later, when it's time to knit the thumb, you will pull out the waste yarn stitches and pick up the open stitches at both the top and the bottom, along with a stitch or two at the sides of the hole.

Kids' Fulled Mittens

When felting processes — hot soapy water, friction, and agitation — are used on knitted fabric, it's called fulling. Fulling shrinks the knit and creates a napped surface. Use sheep's wool or wool-and-mohair blends, not preshrunk or superwashed, treated wools, which don't full properly. The mitten pictured was knit with yarn listed below; you may use any yarn that will provide the required gauge.

Sizes

Child's 2–3 years, 4–6 years, 6–8 years

Yarn

mc: 1 skein tweed red (#0738) Reynolds Lopi, bulky weight, 100% wool

cc A: 10 yds (9m) orange Peace Fleece, worsted weight, 60% wool/40% mohair

cc B: 15 yds (13.5m) Amethyst Brown Sheep Lamb's Pride, bulky weight, 85% wool/15% mohair

Needles

One set #6 (4mm) dp needles, for ribbing

One set #8 (5mm) dp needles, *or size you need to knit correct gauge*

Gauge

4 sts = 1"/2.5cm, larger needles in St st

Other supplies

Two dishpans; real soap, shampoo, or Murphy's Oil Soap; washboard; scrub brush, fine wire brush, or pet comb; stitch holder; washing machine; yarn needle

---

cc = contrast color ◆ **dp** = double point ◆ **K** = knit ◆ **K2tog** = knit 2 together ◆ **mc** = main color ◆ **P** = purl **rnd(s)** = round(s) ◆ **ssk2tog** = slip, slip, knit 2 together **st(s)** = stitch(es) **St st** = stockinette stitch

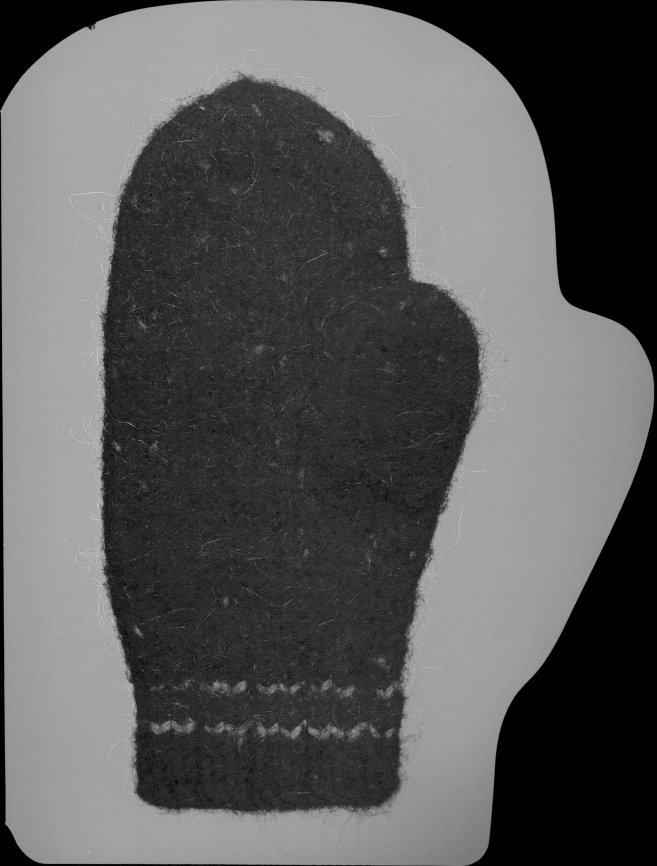

SIZES	2–3 YRS	4–6 YRS	6–8 YRS
Hand length	4½"	5½"	6"
Thumb length	1½"	1¾"	2"
Hand circumference, including thumb tip	5½"	6"	7"
Knitted mitten length	7½"	9"	9½"
Knitted thumb length	1¾"	2¼"	2½"
Knitted mitten width	3⅓"	3½"	4"
Fulled mitten length	6½"	7½"	8"
Fulled thumb length	1½"	1¾"	2"
Fulled mitten width	2¾"	3"	3½"
RIBBING THE CUFF			
With mc and smaller needles, cast on	24 sts	27 sts	30 sts

Distribute sts evenly on three dp needles:
    On Needle 1:
    On Needle 2:
    On Needle 3:
	6 sts
	9 sts
	9 sts
		9 sts
		9 sts
		9 sts
			9 sts
			9 sts
			12 sts

Join in rnd; do not twist the sts.			
Rounds 1–6: *K2, P1; repeat from * to end of rnd.			
Round 7: With cc A, *K2, P1; repeat from * to end of rnd.			
Rounds 8–11: With cc B, *K2, P1; repeat from * to end of rnd.			
Round 12: With cc A, *K2, P1; repeat from * to end of rnd.			
With mc, continue working K2, P1 ribbing until work measures	1¾"	2¼"	2½"
MAKING THUMB GORE AND THUMB HOLE (Right Mitten)			
Round 1: Change to larger needles and St st. With mc, knit to end of rnd.			

	2–3 YRS	4–6 YRS	6–8 YRS
Round 2: K1, M1, knit to end of rnd.			
Rounds 3 and 4: Knit to end of rnd.			
Repeat Rounds 2–4	2 more times	3 more times	4 more times
You will have	27 sts	31 sts	35 sts
Knit even until work measures	3½"	4½"	4¾"
Next Round: K1. Place on a stitch holder the next	6 sts	7 sts	8 sts
Cast on 3 sts over the thumb hole. Knit even to end of rnd. You will have	24 sts	27 sts	30 sts

Distribute sts evenly on three dp needles:
    On Needle 1:
    On Needle 2:
    On Needle 3:
	8 sts
	8 sts
	8 sts
		9 sts
		9 sts
		9 sts
			10 sts
			10 sts
			10 sts

Knit even until work measures	5¾"	7⅓"	8"
MAKING THUMB GORE AND THUMB HOLE (Left Mitten)			
Round 1: Change to larger needles and St st. With mc, knit to end of rnd.			
Round 2	K23, M1, K1	K26, M1, K1	K29, M1, K1
Rounds 3 and 4: Knit to end of rnd.			
Repeat Rounds 2–4	2 more times	3 more times	4 more times
You will have	27 sts	31 sts	35 sts
Knit even until work measures	3½"	4½"	4¾"
Next Round: Knit around to	7 sts before end of third needle	8 sts before end of third needle	9 sts before end of third needle
Place on stitch holder	6 sts	7 sts	8 sts

	2–3 YRS	4–6 YRS	6–8 YRS
Cast on 3 sts over the thumb hole. Knit the last st. You will have	24 sts	27 sts	30 sts
Distribute sts evenly on three dp needles: On Needle 1: On Needle 2: On Needle 3:	8 sts 8 sts 8 sts	9 sts 9 sts 9 sts	10 sts 10 sts 10 sts
Knit even until work measures	5¾"	7⅓"	8"
DECREASING THE MITTEN TIP			
Round 1: *K2tog at both ends of all three needles.			
Rounds 2 and 3: Knit to end of rnd.			
Rounds 4–6: Repeat Rounds 1–3. You will have	12 sts	15 sts	18 sts
Repeat Rounds 1–3	0 more times	1 more time	1 more time
You will have	12 sts	9 sts	12 sts
Break yarn. With yarn needle, draw up remaining sts on yarn end. Thread yarn through sts again, and pull firmly to close. Draw end to inside of mitten.			
KNITTING THE THUMB			
Pick up from the stitch holder	6 sts	7 sts	8 sts
Pick up 3 sts from the cast-on edge at the top of the thumb hole.			
Pick up the sides of corner sts, twisting them as you place them on the needle. Take from each corner	1 st	1 st	1, 2 sts
You will have	11 sts	12 sts	14 sts
Round 1: Knit to end of rnd.			
Round 2: Knit around; K2tog at	1 corner	1 corner	both corners
You will have	10 sts	11 sts	12 sts

	2–3 YRS	4–6 YRS	6–8 YRS
Knit in rnds until thumb length measures	5"	6¼"	7"
DECREASING THE THUMB TIP			
Round 1: Ssk2tog at beginning of all three needles.			
Round 2: Knit around.			
Repeat Rounds 1 and 2 until there remain	7 sts	8 sts	9 sts
Break yarn. With yarn needle, draw up remaining sts on yarn end. Thread yarn through sts again, and pull firmly to close. Draw end to inside mitten.			

Fulling Your Mittens

Full both mittens at the same time, taking turns between them throughout the process. Use the following directions, or wash both mittens in your washing machine with a full load of whites in hot water. When finished, brush thoroughly toward the tips, then air-dry or toss in the dryer with other clothes.

1. Fill one dishpan with very cold water and another with very hot water (as close to boiling as your hands can tolerate).

2. Apply soap to the mitten. Submerse the mitten in hot water, then rub it on the washboard, continually dipping it into the hot water as you work it. Add soap as needed.

3. After a few minutes of scrubbing, plunge the mitten into the cold water, squeezing it quickly to shock it. Let it rest in the cold water while working the other mitten.

4. Repeat steps 2 and 3 until the mittens have fulled as desired. You'll notice that the mittens no longer relax when put back into the hot water, and they will be 16 to 20% shorter and 10% narrower.

5. Rinse the mittens one more time. Using a scrub brush or pet comb (pet slicker), brush thoroughly toward the tip on both sides. Optionally, turn the mittens wrong side out as well, and brush the inside widthwise.

6. Spin the mittens in a washing machine to remove the excess water.

7. Again brush the mittens. Air-dry or toss in a dryer with other clothes.

Skier's Finger Mitts

This is the ultimate glove/mitten cross, with the index finger free to adjust ski bindings, dial a cell phone, or play chopsticks on a cold piano. If the index finger gets cold, it can snuggle with the others in the three-finger pocket. The mitten pictured was knit with yarn listed below; you can use any yarn that will provide the required gauge. This pattern is adapted from a finger mitt by Harriet Pardy Martin.

Sizes

Child's 8–10 yrs, Women's medium, Men's medium

Yarn

Brown Sheep Lamb's Pride, worsted weight, 85% wool/15% mohair

mc: 2 skeins Blue Heirloom

cc A: 1 skein Limeade

cc B: 20 yds Emerald Fantasy

cc C: 20 yds Dynamite Blue

cc D: 5 yds Orange You Glad

cc E: 10 yds Fuschia

Needles

One set #4 (3.5mm) dp needles, *or size you need to knit correct gauge*

Gauge

6½ sts = 1" (2.5cm) in Salt and Pepper

Other supplies

36" (90cm) waste yarn, yarn needle

---

cc = contrast color ◆ **dp** = double point ◆ **Inc** = increase **K** = knit ◆ **K2tog** = knit 2 together ◆ **M1** = make 1 **M1L** = make 1 left-slanted increase ◆ **M1R** = make 1 right-slanted increase ◆ **mc** = main color ◆ **P** = purl ◆ **rnd(s)** = round(s) ◆ **ssk2tog** = slip, slip, knit 2 together ◆ **st(s)** = stitch(es)

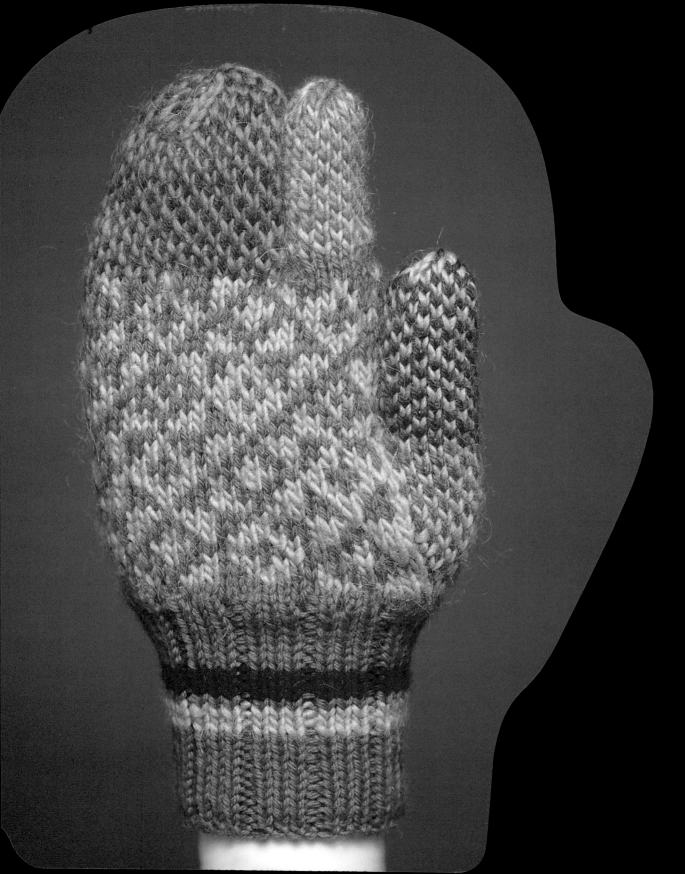

SIZES	8–10 YRS	WOMEN'S M	MEN'S M
Hand length	6½"	7½"	7½"
Thumb length	2¼"	2½"	2½"
Hand circumference, including thumb tip	8"	9"	9½"
Finished mitten length	8¾"	10"	10"
Finished thumb length	2¼"	2½"	2½"
Finished mitten width	3"	3½"	4¼"
RIBBING THE CUFF			
With mc, cast on	36 sts	40 sts	44 sts

Distribute the sts on three dp needles:
    On Needle 1:
    On Needle 2:
    On Needle 3:
	
	12 sts
	12 sts
	12 sts
		
		12 sts
		12 sts
		16 sts
			
			12 sts
			16 sts
			16 sts

Join in rnd, being careful not to twist sts. Use cast-on tail as marker for beginning and end of rnds.			
Rounds 1–10: *K3, P1; repeat from * to end of rnd. Do not break mc; carry it behind work when not in use.			
Rounds 11–13: Join cc A; continue in ribbing with cc A. Break cc A and weave in tail.			
Round 14: Continue in ribbing with mc.			
Rounds 15–17: Join cc E; continue in ribbing with cc E. Break cc E and weave in tail.			
Rounds 18–26: Continue in ribbing with mc.			
STARTING THE HAND			

With mc, begin stockinette stitch. Inc in Round 1 by M1 between knit sts of ribbing:
    On Needle 1:
    On Needle 2:
    On Needle 3:
	
	4 times
	4 times
	4 times
		
		5 times
		5 times
		6 times
			
			6 times
			7 times
			7 times

You will have	48 sts	56 sts	64 sts

SETTING UP THE PATTERNS	8–10 YRS	WOMEN'S M	MEN'S M

Keeping the beginning of the rnd in the same place, distribute sts on three needles:
    On Needle 1:
    On Needle 2:
    On Needle 3:
	12 sts
	12 sts
	24 sts
		14 sts
		14 sts
		28 sts
			16 sts
			16 sts
			32 sts

NOTE: With mc and cc A, you will work the Salt and Pepper pattern and form the thumb gore on Needles 1 and 2 and the Diamonds pattern on Needle 3 (see charts, page 61). Read each line from right to left, starting with Line 1 at the bottom at the point marked for your size. Carry cc A ahead.			
KNITTING PATTERNS AND THUMB GORE *(Right Mitten)*			
Round 1 Needle 1: K1 cc A (marking st), K5 sts Salt and Pepper, K2 cc A (marking sts), *K1 mc, K1 cc A; repeat from * to end of needle in Salt and Pepper pattern. **NOTE:** The first cc A st marks the entrance to the thumb gore. Maintain it in cc A up to the thumb hole. The last 2 cc A sts mark the exit from the thumb gore. Maintain them in cc A up to the thumb hole. The 5 Salt and Pepper sts are the base of the thumb gore. Needle 2: Continue in Salt and Pepper to end of needle. Needle 3: Work first line of Diamond pattern with mc and cc A, starting at lower right and point marked for your size.			
Round 2 Needle 1: K1 cc A, M1L (page 89) maintaining color sequence, knit in Salt and Pepper to next marking st, M1R, K2 cc A, work to end of needle in Salt and Pepper. Needle 2: Work in Salt and Pepper pattern to end of needle. Needle 3: Work in Diamond pattern to end of needle.			

	8–10 YRS	WOMEN'S M	MEN'S M
Repeat Round 2	3 more times	4 more times	6 more times
Between the marking sts, you will have	13 sts	15 sts	19 sts
Needle 1 contains	20 sts	24 sts	30 sts
Maintain cc A marking sts and knit even in established patterns, until work above cuff measures	2¼"	2½"	2½"
MAKING THE THUMB HOLE *(Right Mitten)*			
NOTE: Convert marking sts to Salt and Pepper in this rnd. Look ahead to the established Salt and Pepper to determine which color to begin with on Needle 1.			
Needle 1: K1, put the thumb gore sts on a piece of waste yarn Using twisted M1 (page 14) and maintaining Salt and Pepper color sequence, cast on 5 sts over the gap. Knit the 2 cc A marking sts in Salt and Pepper. Knit to the end of needle in pattern. Needles 2 and 3: Knit across in patterns.	13 sts	15 sts	19 sts
Continue knitting rnds in pattern as established, until length above opening is	1¾"	2"	2"
KNITTING PATTERNS AND THUMB GORE *(Left Mitten)*			
Round 1 Needle 1: Set up Salt and Pepper pattern: *K1 mc, K1 cc A; repeat from * to end of needle. Needle 2: Continue in Salt and Pepper pattern from Needle 1 for K2 cc A (marking sts), K5 sts in Salt and Pepper, K1 cc A (marking st).	4 sts	6 sts	8 sts

	8–10 YRS	WOMEN'S M	MEN'S M
NOTE: The 2 cc A sts mark the entrance to the thumb gore. Maintain them in cc A to the thumb hole. The 5 Salt and Pepper sts between the marking sts are the base of the thumb gore. The last cc A st marks the exit from the thumb gore. Maintain it in cc A up to the thumb hole. Needle 3: Work first line of Diamonds chart using mc and cc A.			
Round 2 Needle 1: Work second line of Salt and Pepper to end of needle. Needle 2: Continue in Salt and Pepper to 2 cc A marking sts. K2 cc A, M1L, knit in Salt and Pepper to the single cc A marking st, M1R, K1 cc A (marking st). Needle 3: Work next line of Diamonds pattern.			
Repeat Round 2	3 more times	4 more times	6 more times
Between the marking sts, you will have	13 sts	15 sts	19 sts
Needle 2 contains	20 sts	24 sts	30 sts
Maintain cc A marking sts and knit even in established patterns, until work above cuff measures	2¼"	2½"	2½"
MAKING THE THUMB HOLE *(Left Mitten)*			
Round 1 Needle 1: Work in pattern to end of needle. Needle 2: Continue in pattern to the marking sts. Convert the cc A marking sts to Salt and Pepper. Put the thumb gore sts on a piece of waste yarn	13 sts	15 sts	19 sts

	8–10 YRS	WOMEN'S M	MEN'S M
Using twisted M1 (page 14) and maintaining Salt and Pepper color sequence, cast on 5 sts over the gap. Knit in pattern to end of needle. (Convert marking sts to Salt and Pepper as you encounter them.) On Needle 2 you will have Needle 3: Knit in Diamonds pattern to end of needle.	12 sts	14 sts	16 sts
Continue knitting even in patterns as established, until length above thumb hole is	1¾"	2"	2"
TAKING OFF THE INDEX FINGER STITCHES *(Right Mitten)*			
Round 1 Needles 1 and 2: Work in pattern to ends of needles. Needle 3: Working in pattern, knit	16 sts	19 sts	22 sts
Place on a piece of waste yarn	8 sts	9 sts	10 sts
Round 2: Place on same waste yarn, first	8 sts	9 sts	10 sts
With twisted M1 and in Salt and Pepper, cast on over the gap	1 st	3 sts	3 sts
Work the remaining sts in the rnd in patterns. In the last 7 sts, join but do not knit cc B. You will have	33 sts	41 sts	47 sts
TAKING OFF THE INDEX FINGER STITCHES *(Left Mitten)*			
Next Round Needle 1: Work Salt and Pepper across needle. Needle 2: In Salt and Pepper pattern, knit	4 sts	5 sts	6 sts
Place on a piece of waste yarn the remaining	8 sts	9 sts	10 sts
Needle 3: Place on same waste yarn the first	8 sts	9 sts	10 sts
With twisted M1 and Salt and Pepper, cast on	1 st	3 sts	3 sts

	8–10 YRS	WOMEN'S M	MEN'S M
Work in pattern the remaining	16 sts	19 sts	22 sts
In the last 7 sts, join back but do not knit with cc B. You will have	33 sts	41 sts	47 sts
COMPLETING THE HAND			
Break mc and cc A; join cc B and cc C. Without moving beginning of rnd, distribute sts on three dp needles: On Needle 1: On Needle 2: On Needle 3:	 11 sts 11 sts 11 sts	 14 sts 14 sts 13 sts	 15 sts 15 sts 17 sts
Knit even in Salt and Pepper on all needles until length above thumb hole measures	3¾"	4"	4"
Decrease Round: On each needle, in pattern, K2tog, knit to last 2 sts on needle, ssk2tog. The pattern should match perfectly at the joins between needles.			
Repeat this decrease every rnd until there remain	9 sts	11 sts	11 sts
Break yarns with 6–8" tails. With yarn needle, thread one tail through remaining sts. Thread tail through sts again and pull closed firmly. Draw both ends to inside of mitten.			
KNITTING THE INDEX FINGER			
From waste yarn, pick up on three needles	16 sts	18 sts	23 sts
From base of the three-finger hand, pick up	1 st	3 sts	3 sts
Pick up 1 st from each corner, twisting it as you place it on the needle. You will have	19 sts	23 sts	27 sts
Distribute these sts as evenly as possible among three dp needles.			
NOTE: Here, join colors by sewing them to the inside face of the fabric, starting at the point where you will begin to knit and sewing away from that point. Pull yarn up so tail is embedded in fabric.			

	8–10 YRS	WOMEN'S M	MEN'S M
Join cc D and knit to end of rnd (for finger ring). *For men's medium only:* K2tog between fingers.			
Break cc D; join cc A and cc B. Knit around in Salt and Pepper, starting from the crotch between finger and hand. At each corner, K2tog in pattern. You will have	17 sts	21 sts	25 sts
Knit even in pattern until work above thumb hole measures	4¼"	4½"	4½"
NOTE: Ideally, try on the figer mitt before decreasing for the fingertip. The work should come halfway up the index finger-nail before decreasing.			
Decrease Round: On each needle, K2tog, knit to last 2 sts on needle, ssk2tog.			
Repeat this decrease every rnd until you have	7 sts	11 sts	9 sts
Break both strands, leaving a 6" tail. Using yarn needle, draw remaining sts up on one strand. Thread tail through sts again and draw up firmly until there is no hole. Draw both strands to inside of mitten.			
KNITTING THE THUMB			
Pick up sts for thumb gore from waste yarn	13 sts	15 sts	19 sts
Pick up 6 sts from the cast-on edge of the thumb hole. Pick up 1 st from each corner of the thumb hole, twisting it as you place it on the needle.			
You will have	21 sts	23 sts	27 sts
Join cc A and cc C. Starting at the corner, work Salt and Pepper on all needles. In first rnd, K2tog in corners to make	19 sts	21 sts	25 sts

	8–10 YRS	WOMEN'S M	MEN'S M
Distribute sts evenly on three dp needles: On Needle 1: On Needle 2: On Needle 3:	6 sts 6 sts 7 sts	7 sts 7 sts 7 sts	8 sts 8 sts 9 sts
Knit even in pattern for	2"	2¼"	2¼"
Decrease Round: *On each needle:* In pattern, K2tog, knit to last 2 sts on needle, ssk2tog.			
Repeat Decrease Round until you have	7 sts	9 sts	7 sts
Break both colors, leaving 6–8" tails. With yarn needle, draw up remaining sts on one yarn end. Thread tail through sts once more and draw up firmly until closed. Draw both tails to inside of mitten. Weave in yarn ends across tip. Stitch together the edges of the hole between the trigger finger and hand. Neatly weave in all ends on the inside.			

Skier's Finger Mitt Charts

Salt and Pepper is worked in several color combinations, as noted in the directions. It is shown here with mc and cc A, as used on the main part of the palm.

mc

cc A

SALT AND PEPPER

Start here

DIAMONDS

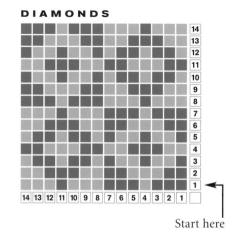

Start here

Chipman's Block

Chipman's Block is an old pattern found by Nova Scotia knitting collector Janetta Dexter. With dry Scottish wit, it isn't quite what it seems. Is it a diagonal gingham check? Look again. Its three-stitch-wide, two-round-high stripes alternate with two rounds of Salt and Pepper seeding. The careful arrangement of these elements creates a grid of solid and speckled diamonds that wraps around the hands, hiding the shaping. The mitten pictured was knit with yarn listed below; you may use any yarn that will provide the required gauge.

Sizes
Child's 6–8 years, Women's small, Women's medium

Yarn
Brown Sheep Nature Spun, worsted weight, 100% wool
mc: 1 skein Sapphire
cc: 1 skein Spring Green

Needles
One set #3 (3.25mm) dp needles, *or size you need to knit correct gauge*
One set #1 (2.25mm) dp needles, for ribbing

Gauge
7½ sts = 1" (2.5cm) on larger needles in Chipman's Block pattern

Other supplies
Stitch holder, stitch marker, yarn needle

---

dp = double point ◆ **inc** = increase ◆ **K** = knit ◆ **K2tog** = knit 2 together ◆ **M1** = make 1 **P** = purl ◆ **rnd(s)** = round(s) **st(s)** = stitch(es)

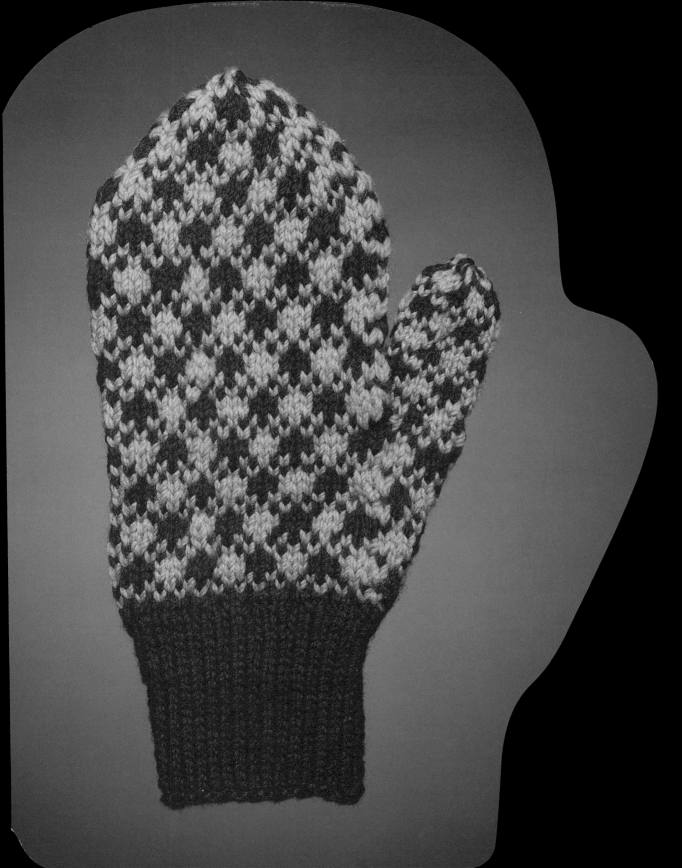

SIZES	6–8 YRS	WOMEN'S S	WOMEN'S M
Hand length	6"	7"	7½"
Thumb length	2"	2⅓"	2½"
Hand circumference above knuckles, including thumb tip	7¼"	8"	9"
Finished mitten length	8"	9⅓"	10"
Finished mitten width	3½"	4"	4½"
Finished thumb length	2"	2⅓"	2½"
RIBBING THE CUFF			
With mc and smaller needles, cast on	48 sts	51 sts	60 sts

Distribute sts on three dp needles:
   On Needle 1:
   On Needle 2:
   On Needle 3:
	15 sts
	18 sts
	15 sts
		15 sts
		18 sts
		18 sts
			18 sts
			21 sts
			21 sts

Join in rnd, being careful not to twist sts.			
Round 1: *K2, P1; repeat from * to end of rnd.			
Continue in K2, P1 ribbing for	2"	2⅓"	2½"
STARTING THE HAND			
Change to larger needles and stockinette stitch.			
Round 1 Needle 1: Knit around, increasing by M1 between the knit stitches of the ribbing, evenly spaced, Needle 2: Repeat Needle 1. Needle 3: Repeat Needle 1. In last 7 sts, join but do not knit cc.	2 times	3 times	2 times
You will have	54 sts	60 sts	66 sts

STARTING THE PATTERN AND THUMB GORE	6–8 YRS	WOMEN'S S	WOMEN'S M
To work Chipman's Block pattern, follow chart (page 69). Read from right to left, starting with Line 1 at the bottom. Repeat the 6-st pattern to the end of each rnd, and repeat the 8 rnds all the way to the tips of the thumb and fingers. Carry the darker color ahead at all times (pages 14–15).			
Round 1 (Line 1 of chart) Needle 1: K1 mc, K1 cc, inc in next st by knitting both colors into 1 st (page 69), place marker, inc 1 in next st by knitting both colors into 1 st as before. Knit to end of the needle in pattern. On Needle 1 you will have	19 sts	20 sts	22 sts
Needles 2 and 3: Knit to end of rnd in pattern. Stitches 2–7 on Needle 1 are the base of the thumb gore.			
Round 2 (Line 2 of chart) Needle 1: K1 cc, K1 mc, *knit both colors into each of the next 2 sts (cc, then mc). Slip marker. Repeat from * once (there is no marker on repeat). Knit to end of needle in pattern. On Needle 1, you will have	23 sts	24 sts	26 sts
Rounds 3 and 4: Work even in pattern.			
Round 5: Knit in pattern to 1 st before marker, knit both colors in next st in pattern, slip marker, knit both colors in next st in pattern, knit to end of rnd in pattern.			
Round 6: Knit in pattern to 2 sts before marker, knit both colors into each of next 2 sts in pattern, slip marker, knit both colors into each of next 2 sts in pattern, knit to end of rnd in pattern. On Needle 1 you will have	29 sts	30 sts	32 sts
Work even in pattern until work above cuff measures	2"	2⅓"	2½"

MAKING THE THUMB HOLE	6–8 YRS	WOMEN'S S	WOMEN'S M
In pattern, K1. Place the next 17 sts on waste yarn. (Discard marker.) With twisted M1 (page 14), cast on 5 sts in pattern over the hole. Continue knitting in pattern to end of rnd. On Needle 1, you will have	17 sts	18 sts	20 sts
Knit even in pattern until work above cuff measures	4¾"	5¼"	5¼"

Finish Line 1 or Line 5 of chart. Redistribute stitches on three dp needles as follows, without moving beginning and end of rnd:
    On Needle 1:
    On Needle 2:
    On Needle 3:
	27 sts
	14 sts
	13 sts
		30 sts
		15 sts
		15 sts
			33 sts
			17 sts
			16 sts

DECREASING FOR THE MITTEN TIP			
Rounds 1–4, *6–8 years size only:* Skip to Round 5.			
Round 1 *Women's small and medium sizes only:* *(Line 2 or 6 of chart)* Needle 1: Knit in pattern to 4 sts before end of needle. K2tog in pattern twice. Needle 2: K2tog in pattern twice; knit in pattern to end of needle. Needle 3: Knit in pattern to end of needle.			
You will have	54 sts	56 sts	62 sts
Round 2 *Women's small and medium sizes only:* Needle 1: Knit in pattern to 2 sts before end of needle, K2tog in pattern. Needle 2: K2tog in pattern. Knit to end of needle. Needle 3: Knit in pattern to end of needle.			
You will have	54 sts	54 sts	60 sts

	6–8 YRS	WOMEN'S S	WOMEN'S M
Rounds 3 and 4 *Women's small and medium sizes only:* Knit even in pattern	42 sts	42 sts	48 sts
Round 5 *(Line 2 or 6 of chart)* Needle 1: K2tog in pattern twice, knit in pattern to 4 sts before end of needle, K2tog in pattern twice. Needle 2: K2tog in pattern twice, knit in pattern to end of needle. Needle 3: Knit in pattern to 4 sts before end of needle, K2tog twice.			
You will have	46 sts	46 sts	52 sts
Round 6 Needle 1: K2tog in pattern, knit to 2 sts before end of needle, K2tog. Needle 2: K2tog in pattern, knit in pattern to end of needle. Needle 3: Knit in pattern to 2 sts before end of needle, K2tog.			
You will have	42 sts	42 sts	48 sts
Round 7–14: Repeat Rounds 3–6 twice more. You will have	18 sts	18 sts	24 sts
Discontinue Chipman's Block pattern and work in Salt and Pepper pattern only.			
Round 15: Work even in Salt and Pepper to end of rnd.			
Round 16: Maintaining pattern, *K1, K2tog; repeat from * to end of rnd. You will have	12 sts	12 sts	16 sts
Break yarn, leaving a 6–8" tail. Draw cc inside mitten. With yarn needle, draw mc yarn through remaining sts. Draw yarn through sts again and pull firmly to close hole. Draw tail inside mitten.			

KNITTING THE THUMB	6–8 YRS	WOMEN'S S	WOMEN'S M
Use size #1 needles for Child's 6–8 years and size #3 needles for Women's small and medium.			
Pick up the 17 thumb gore sts from holder.			
Pick up 5 sts from cast-on edge.			
Pick up 1 st from each corner, twisting the sts as you place them on the needle. You will have 24 sts. Distribute sts evenly on three dp needles, starting with a corner stitch.			
Starting at the right corner, work even in Chipman's Block pattern until thumb measures about	1¾"	2"	2¼"
In the next Salt and Pepper rnd, *K1, K2tog; repeat from * to end of rnd. You will have	16 sts	16 sts	16 sts
Next 2 Rounds: Repeat last rnd, ending K1. You will have	11 sts	11 sts	11 sts
Next Round: Work even in Salt and Pepper.			
Break yarn, leaving a 6–8" tail. Draw cc to inside. With yarn needle, thread mc through remaining sts. Thread the yarn through the sts again and pull firmly to close. Draw tail inside mitten.			
FINISHING			
Draw all ends to the inside of the mitten. Turn mitten inside out, and darn all loose ends into wrong side of fabric. Make another mitten.			

Chipman's Block Chart

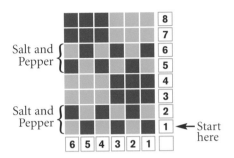

Working in Chipman's Block

Chipman's block is a six-stitch, eight-round repeat, worked on both hand and thumb all the way to the tip. To knit Chipman's Block, follow the chart above. Read each line from right to left, starting with Line 1 at the bottom. Repeat the six-stitch pattern to the end of each round. **NOTE:** Carry the darker color ahead at all times (see page 15).

The rounds with a two-stitch alternation of main color and contrasting color are the Salt and Pepper pattern. All increases occur in these rounds. To increase while maintaining the Salt and Pepper color order, throw one color, then the other, over the needle knitwise, and then draw the two yarns through the stitch on the needle at once. Take care to use the colors in order. In this pattern, there will be 2 mc or 2 cc stitches together at the point where Salt and Pepper rounds end and begin.

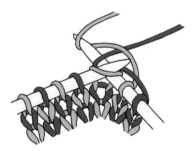

Knitting two colors in one stitch

Peek-a-Boo Mittens

Although these little mittens are knitted on size #2 needles at a tension of 10½ stitches per inch, they won't take a good knitter more than a few hours to make. Even beginners should give them a try: The pattern is simple, the increases and decreases are of an elementary sort, and the mittens are tiny. The mittens pictured were knit with yarn listed below; you may use any yarn that will provide the required fine gauge, which creates a soft but firm fabric. This pattern is copied from a pair of privately owned, antique baby mittens in Brunswick, Maine.

Sizes

6–12 months, 18–24 months,
    3–4 years

Yarn

Rauma Babygarn, fingering weight,
    100% merino wool
mc: 1 skein pink (#B56)
cc: 1 skein blue (#B67)

Needle

One set #2 (2.75mm) dp needles, *or
    size you need to knit correct gauge*

Gauge

10½ sts = 1" (2.5cm) in Stripes pattern

Other supplies

Stitch holder, stitch marker, yarn
    needle

---

cc = contrast color ◆ **dp** = double point ◆ **inc** = increase ◆ **K** = knit
K2tog = knit 2 together ◆ **mc** = main color ◆ **P** = purl ◆ **rnd(s)** =
round(s) ◆ **ssk2tog** = slip, slip, knit 2 together ◆ **st(s)** = stitch(es)

SIZES	6–12 MOS	18–24 MOS	3–4 YRS
Hand length	3⅜"	3½"	4"
Thumb length	1⅛"	1¼"	1⅓"
Hand circumference	About 5"	About 5½"	5½"
Finished mitten length	4½"	4¾"	5½"
Finished thumb length	1¼"	1⅜"	1½"
Finished mitten width	2½"	2⅝"	2¾"
KNITTING THE CUFF			
With mc, cast on	48 sts	54 sts	60 sts

Distribute sts on three dp needles for Peek-a-Boo pattern (3-st repeat):
    On Needle 1:
    On Needle 2:
    On Needle 3:
	
	15 sts
	18 sts
	15 sts
		
		18 sts
		18 sts
		18 sts
			
			18 sts
			24 sts
			18 sts

Join in rnd, being careful not to twist sts.			
Round 1: Join cc in first 3 sts. Work Peek-a-Boo chart (page 77) around needles, reading from right to left, starting at bottom right. Carry mc ahead. Work Lines 1–6	2 times	2 times	2½ times
SETTING UP THE STRIPES AND INCREASING FOR THE THUMB GORE			
For information about the stripe pattern that begins here, please refer to "Two-for-One Increase" on page 73.			
Round 1: Follow the Stripes chart (page 77), beginning with cc. Knit to the last 5 sts in the rnd. Place marker on right needle. Inc in pattern in the next 2 sts by knitting both colors in each st (page 99). Knit the last 3 sts in pattern (mc, cc, mc).			

	6–12 MOS	18–24 MOS	3–4 YRS
Round 2: Working in Stripes pattern, knit to marker (7 sts before end of rnd). Slip marker. Work 2-for-1 increase (below) in next st (mc). Knit in pattern to last 3 sts in rnd. Work 2-for-1 increase in next st (mc). Knit the last 2 sts in pattern (cc, mc). Between the marker and end of rnd you will have	11 sts	11 sts	11 sts
Round 3: Knit even in pattern.			

Two-for-One Increase

The Stripes pattern is a two-stitch alternation of two colors knitted in the round on an even number of stitches, with the same color always carried ahead. It will wrap seamlessly around the hand and pull up the knit in ridges, making a tighter fabric than is possible with single-strand knitting. The color that is carried ahead will be the one that stands out (see pages 14–15).

The two-for-one increases are all made in the main-color stripes, and they make the thumb gore look like a little tree branching out from the cuff. Increases for the thumb begin in the first round. You can increase two stitches within a vertical stripe without interrupting the pattern. Here the increase is made in the dark stripe, resulting in a little dark "Y" with a contrasting stitch in the center.

1. Insert the tip of the right needle knitwise into the stitch below the next stitch on the left needle.
2. Wrap first the dark yarn, then the contrasting yarn, over the tip of the right needle, carrying ahead the same color as you have been. Knit these as a stitch.
3. Knit the dark stitch still on the left needle with the dark yarn.

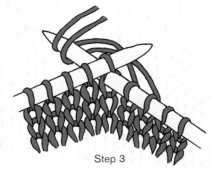

Step 3

	6–12 MOS	18–24 MOS	3–4 YRS
Next Round: *Size 3–4 Years only:* Knit to marker. Work 2-for-1 increase in next st (mc). Knit in pattern to last 3 sts in rnd. Work 2-for-1 increase in the next st (mc). Knit the last 2 sts in pattern (cc, mc).			
All Sizes: There are no more increases. Between marker and end of Needle 3 you will have	11 sts	11 sts	15 sts
Next Rounds: Knit even in pattern until work above cuff measures	1⅛"	1¼"	1⅓"
MAKING THE THUMB HOLE			
Knit in pattern to 1 st before marker. Place this st (cc) on a holder. Discard marker. Place on same holder for the thumb gore the next	11 sts	11 sts	15 sts
Cast on 5 sts in pattern over the gap. K1 mc. Maintain the distribution of stitches as set up for knitting the cuff, as follows: On Needle 1: On Needle 2: On Needle 3:	 15 sts 18 sts 15 sts	 18 sts 18 sts 18 sts	 18 sts 24 sts 18 sts
Knit even in pattern until work above cuff measures	2¼"	2½"	2⅓"
DECREASING THE MITTEN TIP			
NOTE: At this point, decide whether this is a right or a left mitten.			
For the left mitten, the sts are already positioned properly, with the thumb gore sts below the end of Needle 3.			

	6–12 MOS	18–24 MOS	3–4 YRS
For the right mitten, move all 7 sts clockwise to get the thumb gore sts below the beginning of Needle 1: Needle 1: Slip 7 sts to Needle 2. Needle 2: Slip 7 sts to Needle 3. Needle 3: Slip 7 sts (above thumb gore) to Needle 1. *For Size 6–12 months only:* Move 1 st from Needle 2 to Needle 1; move 1 st from Needle 2 to Needle 3. *For Size 3–4 years only:* Move 2 sts from Needle 2 to Needle 1; move 2 sts from Needle 2 to Needle 3.			
For the following decrease, sts should now be distributed as follows, with all needles beginning with an mc st: On Needle 1: On Needle 2: On Needle 3:	 15 sts 18 sts 15 sts	 18 sts 18 sts 18 sts	 18 sts 24 sts 18 sts
Round 1: *On each needle,* K2tog in cc, knit in pattern to end of needle. **NOTE:** After Round 1, there will be 2 cc sts facing each other at the ends of all needles.			
Round 2: *On each needle,* knit in pattern to 2 sts before end of needle, ssk2tog in mc.			
Round 3: *On each needle,* K2tog in mc, knit in pattern to end of needle. **NOTE:** After Round 3, there will be 2 mc sts facing each other at the ends of all needles.			
Round 4: *On each needle,* knit to 2 sts before end of needle, ssk2tog in cc.			
Repeat Rounds 1–4 until 12 sts remain.			

FINISHING	6–12 MOS	18–24 MOS	3–4 YRS
Break yarn. Draw cc yarn to inside mitten. With yarn needle, thread mc yarn tail through remaining sts. Thread yarn through again and pull firmly to close. Draw yarn through to inside mitten.			
KNITTING THE THUMB			
Pick up from holder	11 sts	11 sts	15 sts
Pick up 5 sts from top of thumb hole.			
Pick up the sides of 2 sts from each corner, twisting them as you put them on the needle. You will have	20 sts	20 sts	24 sts

Tips for Two-Color Knitting

- Carry ahead the color you want to emphasize.
- Take the carried-ahead color from under and to the left of the other color.
- Carry the same color ahead throughout a project.
- Carry the darkest color ahead, except when working patterns with fine light lines or light specks.
- When knitting from two balls of yarn, wind center-pull balls to keep them in hand.

	6–12 MOS	18–24 MOS	3–4 YRS
Start knitting on the stitch after the palm-side corner, matching pattern to that on the palm above it. At the corner you should encounter 2 mc sts together. Knit both colors in the first st (mc, cc). Continue across the thumb gore portion, matching stripes to the other corner, where you will again meet 2 mc sts together. K1 mc, then knit both colors (cc, mc) into the next st. You will have	22 sts	22 sts	26 sts
Knit even in pattern for	1"	1"	1¼"
Decrease exactly as on hand until there remain	8 sts	8 sts	6 sts
Break yarn. Draw cc yarn to inside mitten. With yarn needle, thread mc yarn tail through remaining sts. Thread yarn through again and pull firmly to close. Draw yarn inside mitten.			

Peek-a-Boo Charts

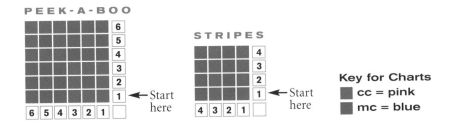

PEEK-A-BOO

6
5
4
3
2
1 ←Start here
6 5 4 3 2 1

STRIPES

4
3
2
1 ←Start here
4 3 2 1

Key for Charts
cc = pink
mc = blue

Covered with Colors

Here is the colorful mitten on this book's cover. The cuff is a traditional Maine, striped stockinette design. The pattern features knits with different tensions – garter stitch, two-colored stranding, plain stockinette, and vertical stripes. Not to worry. If you get 6 stitches per inch in plain stockinette, the rest should fall into place. The mitten pictured was knit with yarn listed below; you may use any yarn that will provide the required gauge.

Sizes

Child's 8–10 years, Adult's small, Adult's medium

Yarn

Brown Sheep Lamb's Pride, worsted weight, 85% wool/15% mohair

cc A: 1 skein Blue Boy
cc B: 1 skein Limeade
cc C: 1 skein Lotus Pink
cc D: 1 skein Emerald Fantasy
cc E: 1 skein Jack's Plum
cc F: 1 skein Orange You Glad

Needles

One set #4 (3.5mm) dp needles, *or size you need to knit correct gauge*

Gauge

6 sts = 1" (2.5cm) in stockinette stitch

Other supplies

Two stitch markers, waste yarn, yarn needle

---

cc = contrast color ◆ **dp** = double point ◆ **K** = knit
K2tog = knit 2 together
M1L = make 1 left-slanted increase ◆ **M1R** = make 1 right-slanted increase
Ssk2tog = slip, slip, knit 2 together ◆ **st(s)** = stitch(es)

SIZES	8–10 YRS	ADULT'S S	ADULT'S M
Hand length	6½"	7"	7½"
Thumb length	2¼"	2⅓"	2½"
Hand circumference, including thumb tip	8"	8"	9"
Finished mitten length	8¾"	9⅓"	10"
Finished thumb length	2¼"	2⅓"	2½"
Finished mitten width	4"	4"	4½"
KNITTING THE CUFF			
With Maine cast-on method (page 10) and cc A, cast on	48 sts	48 sts	52 sts

Distribute sts on three dp needles:
  On Needle 1:
  On Needle 2:
  On Needle 3:
	24 sts
	12 sts
	12 sts
		24 sts
		12 sts
		12 sts
			26 sts
			14 sts
			12 sts

Join in rnd, being careful not to twist sts.			
NOTE: Join each new color by either sewing or knitting over and under it for 7 sts just before it is needed (page 12). When you are finished with a color, weave it in for 7 sts and break or cut it. Later you can trim these woven-in ends without further darning in.			
Rounds 1–3: With cc A, work garter st band: Knit 1 rnd, purl 1 rnd, knit 1 rnd.			
Round 4: Join cc B by sewing. Carrying cc A ahead (pages 14–15), work vertically striped cuff: *K2 cc A, K2 cc B; repeat from * to end of rnd.			
Repeat Round 4 until work measures or about	2¼" 14 rnds	2⅓" 16 rnds	2½" 18 rnds
Next 4 Rounds: Join cc C and with cc C, work a second garter st band: [purl 1 rnd, knit 1 rnd] twice.			
Next Round: Join cc D, and knit 1 rnd. In last 7 sts of rnd, join cc E.			

INCREASING FOR THE THUMB GORE *(Right Mitten)*	8–10 YRS	ADULT'S S	ADULT'S M
NOTE: Here, begin working Chart 1 (page 85) and, *at the same time,* begin increasing at the thumb gore. Read the chart from right to left, starting at Line 1. Repeat 4-st pattern to end of rnd, except at the thumb gore, where you use the Thumb Gore chart for your size (page 85). Weave in cc C and cc F wherever floats are more than 3 sts (page 39). See page 89 for M1L and M1R.			
Join cc E and knit	1 rnd	2 rnds	3 rnds
Work Chart 1 and Thumb Gore chart for the next 11 rnds.			
Round 1 (increase rnd): Starting with Line 1 of Thumb Gore chart for your size, K1, M1L, K3, M1R, place marker, knit to end of rnd. The marker signals the beginning of the Thumb Gore chart.			
Round 2: Continuing Chart 1 and Thumb Gore chart, knit even in pattern to end of rnd.			
Round 3 (increase rnd): K1, M1L, work Thumb Gore chart to marker, M1R, slip marker. Follow Chart 1 to end of rnd.			
Rounds 4–10: Repeat Rounds 2–3, ending with Round 2.			
Round 11: Finish Thumb Gore chart for your size, then	knit even	knit even	repeat Round 3
Knit with cc E	1 rnd	2 rnds	3 rnds
You will have	58 sts	58 sts	64 sts
Between the first st in rnd and the marker, there are	13 sts	13 sts	15 sts
Join cc D and knit 1 rnd.			
Join cc A and knit 1 rnd, then purl 1 rnd.			

MAKING THE THUMB HOLE *(Right Mitten)*	8–10 YRS	ADULT'S S	ADULT'S M
With cc A, K1, place on waste yarn the thumb gore sts	13 sts	13 sts	15 sts
Using the twisted M1 (page 14), cast on 3 sts over the gap. Knit to end of rnd in cc A. You will have	48 sts	48 sts	52 sts
INCREASING FOR THE THUMB GORE *(Left Mitten)*			
NOTE: Here, you begin working Chart 1 (page 85) and, *at the same time,* begin increasing at the thumb gore. Read the chart from right to left, starting at Line 1, and repeat the 4-st pattern to the end of rnd, except at the thumb gore, where you use the Thumb Gore chart for your size (page 85). Weave in cc C and cc F wherever floats are more that 3 sts (page 39).			
Join cc E and knit	1 rnd	2 rnds	3 rnds
Work Chart 1 and Thumb Gore chart for the next 11 rnds.			
Round 1 (increase rnd): Starting with Line 1 of chart, knit to 4 sts before end of rnd. Place marker. M1L, K3, M1R, K1. The marker signals the beginning of the Thumb Gore chart. See page 89 for M1L and M1R.			
Round 2: Continue Chart 1 and Thumb Gore chart; knit even in pattern to end of rnd.			
Round 3 (increase rnd): Knit to marker, slip marker, M1L, work Thumb Gore chart to 1 st before end of needle, M1R, K1.			
Rounds 4–10: Repeat Rounds 2 and 3, ending with Round 2.			
Round 11: Finish Thumb Gore chart for your size, then	knit even	knit even	repeat Round 3
Knit with cc E	1 rnd	2 rnds	3 rnds
You will have	58 sts	58 sts	64 sts

	8–10 YRS	ADULT'S S	ADULT'S M
On Needle 3, between the marker and the last st on needle, you will have	13 sts	13 sts	15 sts
Join cc D and knit 1 rnd.			
Join cc A. Knit 1 rnd, then purl 1 rnd.			
MAKING THE THUMB HOLE *(Left Mitten)*			
With cc A, knit to marker. Discard marker.			
Place on waste yarn	13 sts	13 sts	15 sts
Using twisted M1 (page 14), cast on 3 sts over the gap, K1. You will have	48 sts	48 sts	52 sts
CONTINUING THE HAND			
With cc A, purl to end of rnd.			
Join cc C. Work Chart 2 (page 85), starting at Line 1 and reading from right to left. Join cc F and cc A as needed, and repeat the 4-st motif to end of each rnd. When chart is completed, join cc D.			
DECREASING THE MITTEN TIP			
Rounds 1–2: With cc D, work third garter-stitch band: Knit 1 rnd, purl 1 rnd.			
Round 3: Knit 1 rnd, decreasing 2 sts by K2tog at *both* ends of Needle 1.			
Round 4: Purl 1 rnd.			
Round 5: Join cc B; knit with it to end of rnd.			
Rounds 6–8: Knit even in cc B.			
Round 9 (decrease rnd) Needle 1: K1, ssk2tog, knit to last 3 sts before end of needle, K2tog, K1. Needle 2: K1, ssk2tog, knit to end of needle. Needle 3: Knit to last 3 sts on needle, K2tog, K1. You will have	42 sts	42 sts	46 sts

	8–10 YRS	ADULT'S S	ADULT'S M
Round 10: Knit even to end of rnd.			
Repeat Rounds 9 and 10 four more times.			
Repeat Round 9	4 times	4 times	5 times
You will have	10 sts	10 sts	10 sts
Break yarn, leaving an 8" tail. With needle, thread yarn end through sts on needle. Thread end through sts again, and pull firmly to close. Draw yarn end inside mitten.			
KNITTING THE THUMB			
Pick up thumb gore sts from waste yarn	13 sts	13 sts	15 sts
Pick up 3 sts along the cast-on edge at the top of the hole.			
Pick up the side of 1 st in each corner of the hole, twisting it as you place it on the needle. You will have	18 sts	18 sts	20 sts
Distribute sts as evenly as possible on three dp needles.			
Round 1: Join cc A and knit with it to end of rnd.			
Round 2: Purl 1 rnd with cc A.			
Round 3: Join cc C by sewing, and knit with it to end of rnd.			
Round 4: Knit to end of rnd, decreasing 1 st at palm side of thumb by K2tog	0 times	0 times	1 time
You will have	18 sts	18 sts	19 sts
Knit even in rnds with cc C until thumb measures	2"	2"	2⅓"
DECREASING THE THUMB TIP			
Round 1: On *each* needle, K2tog, knit to 2 sts before end of needle, ssk2tog. You will have	12 sts	12 sts	13 sts

	8-10 YRS	ADULT'S S	ADULT'S M
Round 2: Knit even.			
Repeat Round 1. You will have	6 sts	6 sts	7 sts
Break yarn, leaving a 6" tail. Using yarn needle, thread yarn end through sts on needle. Thread end through sts again, and pull firmly to close hole. Pull end inside mitten and weave in end.			
FINISHING THE MITTEN			
Turn mitten inside out, work in loose tails, and trim worked-in tails close to fabric. Knit a second mitten for the other hand.			

Covered with Colors Charts

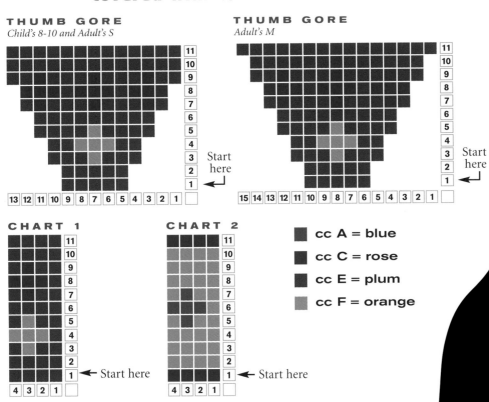

THUMB GORE
Child's 8-10 and Adult's S

THUMB GORE
Adult's M

Start here

Start here

CHART 1

← Start here

CHART 2

← Start here

cc A = blue

cc C = rose

cc E = plum

cc F = orange

85

Nepalese Mittens

The original design for this project came from an anonymous knitter in Nepal who understood what it takes to make a warm and handsome mitten. A thick hem lines the cuff all the way to the base of the thumb, and hand-stitching pulls it in snug to the wrist. The thumb lies flat to the side of the mitten, making left and right mittens interchangeable. The mitten pictured was knit with yarn listed below; you may use any yarn that will provide the required gauge.

Sizes
Women's medium, Men's medium, Men's large

Yarn
Brown Sheep Lamb's Pride, worsted weight, 85% wool/15% mohair
mc: 1–2 skeins Deep Charcoal
cc A: 1 skein Emerald Fantasy
cc B: 100 yds Lotus Pink

Needles
One set #8 (5mm) dp needles, *or size you need to knit correct gauge*

Gauge
4 sts = 1" (2.5cm) in stockinette stitch

Other supplies
Stitch holder, two stitch markers, 12" (30cm) waste yarn, yarn needle

---

cc = contrast color ◆ **dp** = double point ◆ **K** = knit
K2tog = knit 2 together
M1L = make 1 left-slanted increase ◆ **M1R** = make 1 right-slanted increase ◆ **mc** = main color ◆ **rnd(s)** = round(s)
ssk2tog = slip, slip, knit 2 together ◆ **st(s)** = stitch(es)

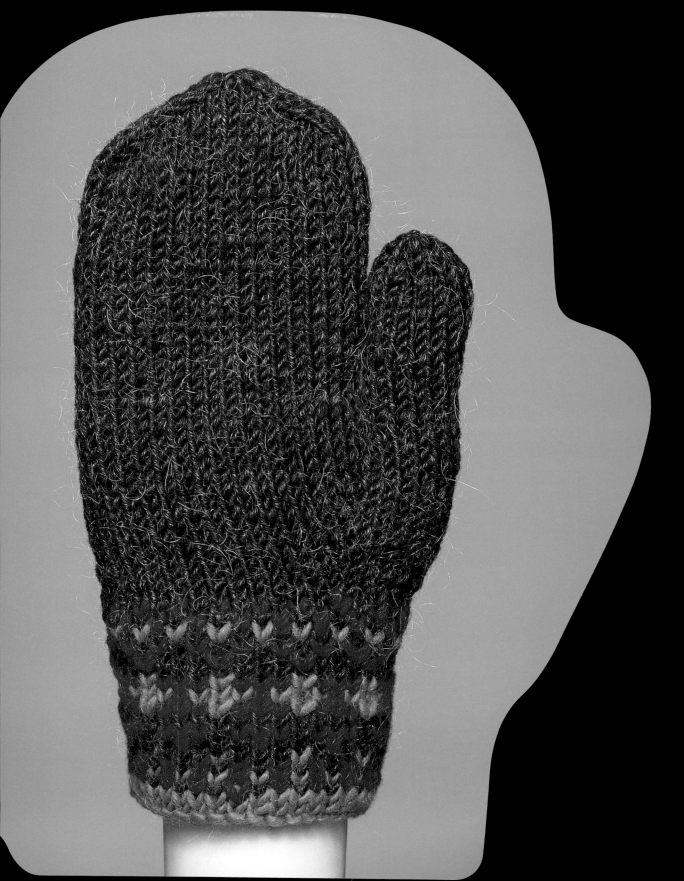

SIZES	WOMEN'S M	MEN'S M	MEN'S L
Hand length	7½"	7½"	9"
Thumb length	2½"	2½"	3"
Hand circumference, including thumb tip	9"	9½"	10"
Finished mitten length	10"	10"	12"
Finished thumb length	2½"	2½"	3"
Finished mitten width	4½"	4¾"	5¼"
MAKING THE FLARED CUFF			
With cc A, cast on	36 sts	38 sts	40 sts

Distribute sts on three dp needles:
    On Needle 1:
    On Needle 2:
    On Needle 3:
	12 sts
	12 sts
	12 sts
		12 sts
		12 sts
		14 sts
			13 sts
			13 sts
			14 sts

Join in rnd, being careful not to twist the sts. Knit in rnds for	2½"	2½"	3"
Next Round: Purl to end of rnd to create the hem edge.			
Next Round: Knit even to end of rnd in cc A. In the same rnd, *for Men's medium only,* increase 2 sts, evenly spaced. (You need a multiple of 4 sts for the pattern.)			
You will have	36 sts	40 sts	40 sts
KNITTING THE PATTERN			
Follow the Nepalese chart (page 91), starting with Line 1 at the bottom and reading each line from right to left. Repeat the 4-st pattern to the end of each rnd. Carry one color, usually the darker color, consistently ahead (pages 14–15) in every two-color rnd of the pattern. Knit the entire chart. Break both cc ends and weave in one in each of the next 2 rnds.			

Increasing Experience

Make 1 right-slanted increase (M1R). Pinch the yarn with your left little and ring fingers (do this even if you knit with the yarn in your right hand). Position your left thumb over the yarn, bring it under the yarn and up toward you (as if scooping a hole in cake icing with your thumbnail). Insert the right needle into the loop knitwise as if your left thumb were a needle, transfer it from your thumb to the needle, and pull it to a comfortable tension on the needle. The next time you encounter it, call it a stitch and knit into the back of it. This increase is twisted counterclockwise and will slant right.

Make 1 left-slanted increase (M1L). This is the mirror image of M1R: Start with the yarn pinched in your right lesser fingers (even if you knit with the yarn in your left hand). This time, position your right thumb over the yarn and scoop under the yarn and toward you with your right thumb, as if scooping a hole in the top of a quart of ice cream. Slip the left side of this onto the right needle knitwise, pull it to a comfortable tension on the needle, and in the next round, knit into the front of it – the side you always knit into. This increase is twisted clockwise and will slant left.

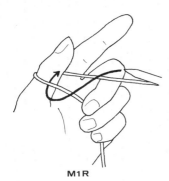

M1R

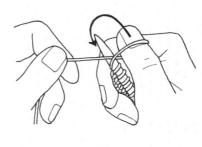

M1L

Right slanting

Left slanting

MAKING ROOM FOR THE THUMB	WOMEN'S M	MEN'S M	MEN'S L
Round 1: With mc, K1, place marker for end of thumb sts, M1L (page 89).			
Knit	23 sts	25 sts	23 sts
M1R, place marker for start of thumb sts, knit	12 sts	14 sts	16 sts
On needles, you will have	38 sts	42 sts	42 sts
Between thumb markers you will have	13 sts	15 sts	17 sts
Round 2: Knit even, slipping markers as you meet them.			
Continue increasing by M1L after the first marker and M1R before the second marker every other row	5 more times	5 more times	8 more times
You will have	48 sts	52 sts	58 sts
Knit 2 rnds even.			
KNITTING THE THUMB			
Slip first st of rnd to Needle 3 (for thumb). Slip onto waste yarn (for hand) next	35 sts	37 sts	41 sts
Divide the thumb sts evenly among three dp needles. You will have	13 sts	15 sts	17 sts
Knit around even until thumb measures	2¼"	2¼"	2¾"
Next Round: K2tog to last st, K1. You will have	7 sts	8 sts	9 sts
Next Round: Knit even to end of rnd.			
Break yarn, leaving a 6–8" tail. With needle, draw up remaining sts on yarn end. Thread tail through sts again; pull firmly to close.			
KNITTING THE HAND			
With three dp needles, pick up sts from holder. Pick up 1 st at base of thumb. You will have	36 sts	38 sts	42 sts

	WOMEN'S M	MEN'S M	MEN'S L
Keeping the single st you picked up at the base of the thumb as the first st on Needle 1, distribute sts on three dp needles: On Needle 1: On Needle 2: On Needle 3:	 18 sts 9 sts 9 sts	 19 sts 10 sts 9 sts	 21 sts 11 sts 10 sts
Knit in rnds until hand, from purl rnd at bottom of cuff, measures	9"	9"	11"
DECREASING FOR MITTEN TIP			
Round 1 Needle 1: K1, ssk2tog, knit to last 3 sts on needle, K2tog, K1. Needle 2: K1, ssk2tog, knit to end of needle. Needle 3: Knit to last 3 sts, K2tog, K1.			
Repeat Round 1 until there remain	12 sts	14 sts	14 sts

Finishing

Break yarn, leaving a 6–8" tail. With yarn needle, draw up remaining stitches on yarn end. Thread yarn through stitches again and pull firmly to close. Draw end to inside of mitten.

Fold bottom of cuff to wrong side along purl ridge. Sew firmly to back of fabric with overhand stitch. Draw up slightly to make a "waist" at top of wrist. Darn all loose ends to inside of mitten and trim.

Knit an identical mitten for the other hand.

NEPALESE CHART

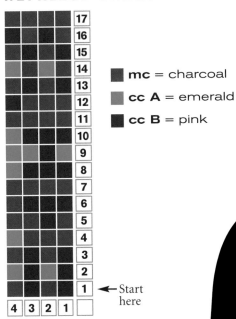

mc = charcoal

cc A = emerald

cc B = pink

← Start here

Labrador Diamonds

In these mittens, interlaced diamonds form *trompe de l'oeil* checkerboards; plaids on the back and simple checks thicken the palm, while main-color lines set off the thumb gore. Always carry the dark color ahead when working the pattern. (See pages 14–15 for carrying yarn ahead.) The mittens pictured were knit with yarn listed below; you may use any yarn that will provide the required gauge.

Sizes

Newborn to 6 months, Child's 3 years

Yarn

Rauma Babygarn, fingering weight,
  100% merino wool
mc: 1 skein lavender (#B96)
cc: 1 skein blue (#B67)

Needles

One set #1 (2.25mm) dp needles, for
  ribbing
One set #2 (2.75mm) dp needles, *or
  size you need to knit correct gauge*

Gauge

9 sts = 1" (2.5cm) in Salt and Pepper
  pattern on larger needles

Other supplies

Stitch holder, 24" (60cm) waste yarn,
  yarn needle

---

cc = contrast color ◆ **dp** =
double point ◆ **inc** = increase
K = knit ◆ **K2tog** = knit 2
together ◆ **M1** = make 1
mc = main color ◆ **P** = purl
rnd(s) = round(s) ◆ **ssk2tog**
= slip, slip, knit 2 together
st(s) = stitch(es)

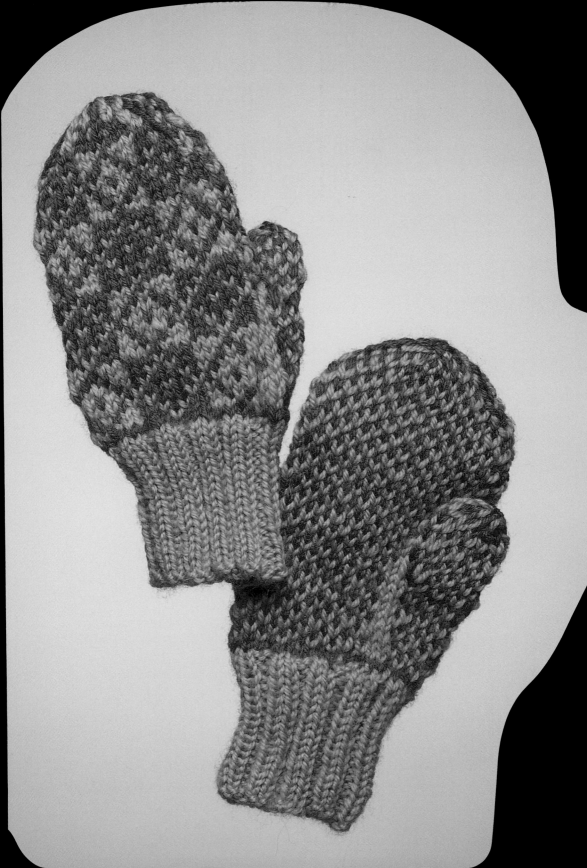

SIZES	TO 6 MOS	3 YEARS
Hand length	3½"	4½"
Thumb length	1⅙"	1½"
Hand circumference, at knuckles, including thumb tip	4"	6"
Finished mitten length	5"	6½"
Finished thumb length	1¼"	1½"
Finished mitten width	2"	3"
RIBBING THE CUFF		
With the smaller needles and mc, cast on	40 sts	54 sts
Join in rnd, being careful not to twist sts.		
Round 1: *K2, P2; repeat from * to end of rnd.		
Continue in K2, P2 rib until the cuff measures	1½"	2"
Change to larger needles and stockinette stitch. With mc [K20, M1] twice; knit even to end of rnd. You will have	42 sts	56 sts
Without moving end of rnd, distribute sts on three dp needles: On Needle 1: On Needle 2: On Needle 3:	 21 sts 10 sts 11 sts	 28 sts 14 sts 14 sts
NOTE: For both the Diamonds and the Salt and Pepper patterns (page 113), consistently carry the same (darker) color ahead (pages 14–15).		

STARTING THE PATTERN AND THUMB GORE (Right Mitten)	TO 6 MOS	3 YEARS
Round 1 Needle 1: Start Diamonds pattern, reading each line from right to left. Starting in the lower right corner at Line 1, knit	21 sts	28 sts
Needles 2 and 3: Start thumb gore and Salt and Pepper pattern: K1 mc (marking st), K1 cc [K1 mc, K1 cc] twice; K2 mc (marking sts). Knit to end of rnd in Salt and Pepper. The 5 sts between the first marking st and the two mc marking sts are the thumb gore sts.		
Round 2 Needle 1: Continue Diamonds pattern. Needles 2 and 3: K1 mc, M1L cc, continue in Salt and Pepper to the 2 mc marking sts, M1R cc. Continue in Salt and Pepper to end of rnd. See page 89 for M1L and M1R.		
Round 3: Knit even in established patterns.		
Next Rounds: Repeat Rounds 2 and 3	2 more times	3 more times
Between (not including) the first and last marking sts, you will have	11 sts	13 sts
On all three needles you will have	48 sts	64 sts
Keeping the two mc thumb gore marking lines, knit even in patterns until work above cuff measures	1⅙"	1½"
Complete Diamonds pattern through	Line 10	Line 14
MAKING THE THUMB HOLE (Right Mitten)		
NOTE: Marking sts are converted to Salt and Pepper in this rnd.		
Round 1 Needle 1: Knit even in Diamonds pattern.		

	TO 6 MOS	3 YEARS
Needles 2 and 3: Maintain Salt and Pepper pattern to first marking st. Knit marking st in Salt and Pepper. Place the thumb gore sts on a piece of waste yarn	11 sts	13 sts
NOTE: Look ahead to the established Salt and Pepper pattern to determine which color to begin with.		
Using twisted M1 (page 14) and Salt and Pepper alternation of colors, cast on 5 sts over the gap. Knit to end of rnd in Salt and Pepper. You will have	42 sts	56 sts
Knit even in patterns until work above cuff measures	2¾"	4¼"
STARTING THE PATTERN AND THUMB GORE *(Left Mitten)*		

Round 1

Needle 1: Start Diamonds pattern, reading each line from right to left, and starting in the lower right corner at Line 1.

Needle 2: Start Salt and Pepper pattern: *K1 mc, K1 cc; repeat from * to end of needle.

Needle 3: Continue Salt and Pepper pattern to 8 sts before end of needle; K2 mc (marking sts), K1 cc [K1 mc, K1 cc] twice; K1 mc (marking st). The 5 sts between the two mc marking sts and the last mc marking st are the thumb gore sts.

Round 2

Needle 1: Continue Diamonds pattern.

Needle 2: Continue Salt and Pepper pattern.

Needle 3: Continue Salt and Pepper pattern to 2 mc marking sts. K2 mc, M1L cc, work Salt and Pepper to last st, M1R in pattern, K1 mc.

Round 3: Knit even in established patterns.

	TO 6 MOS	3 YEARS
Next Rounds: Repeat Rounds 2 and 3	2 more times	3 more times
Between (not including) the first and last marking sts, you will have	11 sts	13 sts
On all three needles, you will have	48 sts	64 sts
Keeping the two mc thumb gore marking lines, knit even in patterns until work above cuff measures	1⅛"	1½"
Complete Diamonds pattern through	Line 10	Line 14

MAKING THE THUMB HOLE *(Left Mitten)*

	TO 6 MOS	3 YEARS
NOTE: Marking sts are converted to Salt and Pepper in this rnd.		
Round 1 Needle 1: Knit even in Diamonds pattern. Needle 2: Knit even in Salt and Pepper. Needle 3: Knit even in Salt and Pepper pattern to first mc marking sts. Knit marking sts in Salt and Pepper. Place the thumb gore sts on a piece of waste yarn	11 sts	13 sts
Using twisted M1 (page 14) and Salt and Pepper alternation of colors, cast on 5 sts over the gap. Knit last st in Salt and Pepper. You will have	42 sts	56 sts
Knit even in patterns until work above cuff measures	2¾"	4¼"

DECREASING THE MITTEN TIP

	TO 6 MOS	3 YEARS
Round 1 Needle 1: Ssk2tog, knit in Diamonds pattern to last 2 sts, K2tog in pattern. Needle 2: Ssk2tog, knit in Salt and Pepper pattern to end of needle. Needle 3: Knit in Salt and Pepper pattern to last 2 sts, K2tog in pattern.		

	TO 6 MOS	3 YEARS
You will have	38 sts	52 sts
Round 2: In patterns, knit to end of rnd.		
Next Rounds: Repeat Round 1	5 more times	9 more times
You will have	18 sts	16 sts
Next Round: Following the pattern as closely as possible, *K1, K2tog; repeat from * to end of rnd. You will have	12 sts	11 sts
Break yarn. Draw cc inside mitten. With needle, thread mc yarn through remaining sts. Draw through sts again. Pull firmly to close.		
Weave in yarn end across tip, inside mitten.		
KNITTING THE THUMB		
From stitch holder, pick up	11 sts	13 sts
In each corner, pick up the side of a st, twisting it as you place it on the needle.		
Pick up 5 sts along the cast-on edge. Divide sts evenly among needles. You will have	18 sts	20 sts
Round 1: Work in Salt and Pepper, decreasing by K2tog at one corner.		
Next Rounds: Work even in pattern until thumb measures	¾"	1¼"
DECREASING THE THUMB TIP		
Next Round: *K2tog; repeat from * to end of rnd.		
Break yarn. Draw cc inside mitten. With needle, thread mc yarn through remaining sts. Draw through sts again. Pull firmly to close.		
FINISHING		
Turn mitten inside out. Darn all loose yarn ends into floats on wrong side of mitten (page 39). Trim ends close to fabric.		

Labrador Diamonds Charts

DIAMONDS

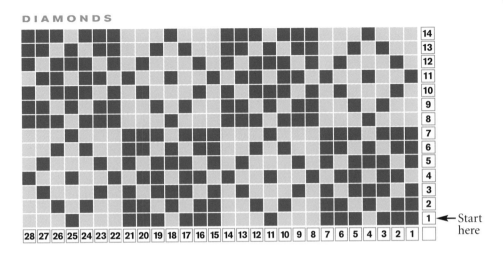

28	27	26	25	24	23	22	21	20	19	18	17	16	15	14	13	12	11	10	9	8	7	6	5	4	3	2	1		

Rows (right side): 14, 13, 12, 11, 10, 9, 8, 7, 6, 5, 4, 3, 2, 1 ← Start here

SALT AND PEPPER

	2
1	← Start here
2	1	

mc = lavender

cc = blue

Knitting Two Colors in One

To make a simple two-strand increase when two or more increases are crowded together, knit both strands into one stitch. Insert the right needle knitwise into the next stitch. Maintaining the pattern's color sequence, wrap first one and then the other color strand around the right needle knitwise, carrying the darker color ahead, as usual. Knit off both together to create two stitches in place of one on the right needle. In the next round, knit each one separately, carefully maintaining any color sequence.

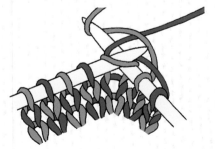

Fisherman's Rib

This is a fisherman's rib, not a fisherman's mitten.
The thick, flexible rib has been used for fishermen's
sweaters in Scotland and Denmark for generations.
This project is for experienced knitters. The increases
and decreases are tricky, and the stitch is slowgoing,
but the resulting mittens are weatherproof and warm.
The one pictured was knit with yarn listed below; you
can use any yarn that will provide the required gauge.

Sizes

Child's small, Child's large, Adult's
medium

Yarn

Rauma Strikkegarn 3-ply, DK weight,
100% wool

3 skeins lime green (#198)

NOTE: Worsted weight works up
into a very rugged mitten; DK
yarn is a lighter weight version.

Needles

One set #2 (2.75mm) straight needles,
for wrist

One set #4 (3.5mm) straight needles,
or size needed to knit correct gauge

One set #4 (3.5mm) dp needles

Gauge

4 sts = 1" (2.5cm) on larger needles
in Fisherman's Rib pattern

Other supplies

Two stitch markers, waste yarn, yarn
needle

---

dp = double point ◆ **K** = knit
K2tog = knit 2 together ◆ **M1**
= make 1 ◆ **P** = purl ◆ **P2tog**
= purl 2 together ◆ **rs** = right
side **ssk2tog** = slip, slip, knit
2 together **ssp2tog** = slip, slip,
purl 2 together ◆ **st(s)** =
stitch(es) ◆ **ws** = wrong side

SIZES	CHILD'S S	CHILD'S L	ADULT'S M
Hand length	4½"	6"	7½"
Thumb length	1½"	2"	2½"
Hand circumference (with thumb)	5"	7"	9"
Finished mitten length	8"	9½"	11½"
Finished thumb length	1½"	2"	2½"
Finished mitten width (pressed flat with ruler)	2¾"	3¾"	4¾"
KNITTING THE CUFF			
Using larger straight needles, cast on	22 sts	30 sts	42 sts
Work Fisherman's Rib pattern (page 103) on all sts until work measures	3"	3"	3"
Change to smaller needles. *P1, K1; repeat from * to end of row, turn. (Include the yarn over with the knit st.)			
Repeat last row 5 more times.			
Change back to larger straight needles and Fisherman's Rib pattern. Work 4 rows (2 right side and 2 wrong side).			
MAKING THE THUMB GORE			
On right side, find the center st and tie a piece of contrasting yarn to it below the knitting needle. This is also the center st of the thumb gore. You will increase in the 2 knit ribs on either side of this marker. A 4-st increase is a 2-row process, starting on the right side.			
Row 1 (rs): Work in Fisherman's Rib up to knit rib before the marker, then increase as follows. (For an illustration of this increase, see page 104.) Yarn forward, knit into the st *beneath* the next knit st, bring new st up, knit the next st on the left needle (you will have 2 knit sts side by side), yarn forward,			

	CHILD'S S	CHILD'S L	ADULT'S M
slip purl st purlwise, K1 (center st), yarn forward, slip purl st purlwise, yarn forward, knit into st *beneath* the next st, bring new st up, knit the next st on the left needle. Continue across row in Fisherman's Rib.			
Row 2 (ws): Work in pattern to the side-by-side purl sts. Yarn forward, slip 1 st purlwise, M1, yarn forward, slip 1 purl-wise, K1 (center st). Repeat this increase between the next 2 side-by-side purl sts. Complete row in pattern. **NOTE:** Next row, treat the 2 knit sts as knit ribs in pattern and purl the M1.			

Knitting Fisherman's Rib

Row 1: The first row after the cast on sets up the Fisherman's Rib. With yarn forward (as if to purl), slip 1 stitch purl-wise. Then, allowing the yarn to go *over* the needle to create a yarn-over, knit the next stitch. Repeat across the row.

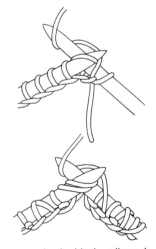

Row 2: On Row 2 and all following rows: With yarn forward, slip 1 stitch as if to purl. As on Row 1, allow the yarn to go *over* the needle, then knit the yarn-over from the previous row together with the next knit stitch. Repeat across row.

NOTE: The stitches you *knit* are the yarn-overs paired with the slipped purl stitches of the preceding row; the stitches you *slip* are the knit stitches of the previous row. When you count stitches, do not count the yarn-overs as a stitch; they are always paired with a knit stitch and the pair should be counted as 1 stitch.

	CHILD'S S	CHILD'S L	ADULT'S M
Repeat this increase in the outermost knit ribs of the thumb gore every second right-side row	0 times	0 times	1 time
In the thumb gore, you will have	5 sts	7 sts	11 sts
On the needles, you will have a total of	26 sts	34 sts	50 sts
Work even in pattern until length from plain ribbing (not counting sts on needle) measures	1½"	2"	2½"

Increasing in Fisherman's Rib

The increases for the thumb gore are made in the stitches on each side of the center stitch. Identify the center stitch by tying a piece of contrasting yarn to the fabric below the knitting needle.

Row 1: Work in Fisherman's Rib to 2 stitches before the center stitch (a knit stitch). Insert your needle into the middle of the stitch beneath the next stitch. Knit a new stitch, then knit the stitch on the needle, together with its yarn over. You will have 2 knit stitches side by side. Continue in Fisherman's Rib to 2 stitches after the center stitch (another knit stitch). As before, knit a stitch into the stitch below the next stitch, then knit the stitch on the needle together with its yarn over.

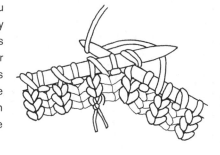

Row 2: Work in Fisherman's Rib until you come to the 2 side-by-side purl stitches. Bring the yarn forward and slip the first purl stitch as if to purl. Then M1 (page 89) in the bar between the purl stitches. Next, bring the yarn forward and slip the second purl stitch as if to purl. Knit 1 (the center stitch). Repeat this increase between the next 2 side-by-side purl stitches.

MAKING THE THUMB HOLE	CHILD'S S	CHILD'S L	ADULT'S M
Row 1: Work in pattern for	11 sts	14 sts	20 sts
Place on waste yarn for the thumb the next	5 sts	7 sts	11 sts
Using twisted M1 (page 14), cast on	3 sts	3 sts	5 sts
Work even in pattern to end of row. You will have	24 sts	30 sts	44 sts
Work even in pattern until hand above "waist" measures	4"	5"	6½"
End with wrong-side row completed.			
DECREASING THE MITTEN TIP			
Row 1 (rs): Still using larger needles, work 1 row in K1, P1 ribbing, converting the Fisherman Rib knit sts to single knit sts. You will have	24 sts	30 sts	44 sts
Mark the center st by tying a piece of contrasting yarn to the fabric beneath the needle.			
Row 2 (ws): P1, P2tog, *K1, P1; repeat from * to 2 sts *before* center st. P2tog, P1, ssp2tog. **NOTE:** The center st and 1 st on each side of it are all purl sts.			
Continue in K1, P1 ribbing until 3 sts remain on needle, P2tog, K1.			
Row 3 (rs): P1, K1, P1, K2tog, continue in ribbing to 3 sts *before* center st, ssk2tog, P1, K1 (center st), P1, K2tog.			
Continue in ribbing until 4 sts remain on needle, ssk2tog, P1, K1.			
You will have	16 sts	22 sts	36 sts
Repeat Rows 2 and 3 until you have	12 sts	10 sts	12 sts

	CHILD'S S	CHILD'S L	ADULT'S M
Break yarn, leaving a 12–14" tail. With yarn needle and starting at the opposite end of the row, thread yarn through remaining sts. Draw yarn end through sts one more time. Pull firmly to close.			
Use the tail to sew the side seam. Fold mitten with wrong side together, aligning the side seam from fingertips to cuff. Work back and forth on the right side, taking up the sides of adjacent stitches, as shown in the illustration on page 107.			

KNITTING THE THUMB

	CHILD'S S	CHILD'S L	ADULT'S M
NOTE: Although you continue to knit back and forth for the thumb, you use several dp needles so that you can knit around corners.			
Row 1: Using dp needles, pick up the thumb gore sts from waste yarn	5 sts	7 sts	11 sts
Pick up from cast-on edge	3 sts	3 sts	5 sts
Pick up the side of 1 st at each corner, twisting it as you place it on the needle.			
Counting yarn overs and knit sts as one, you will have	10 sts	12 sts	18 sts
Distribute sts so row starts at a corner and join yarn.			
Continue pattern from thumb gore, working back and forth in rows until thumb is	1½"	1¾"	2"
You may also measure from the top of the wrist ribbing	3"	3¾"	4½"
End with wrong-side row completed.			

DECREASING THE THUMB

	CHILD'S S	CHILD'S L	ADULT'S M
Row 1 (rs): Change to K1, P1 ribbing, matching knit and purl sts from Fisherman's Rib. Work ribbing to end of row.			

	CHILD'S S	CHILD'S L	ADULT'S M
Row 2 (ws) *Sizes Child's S and Child's L only:* Work rib to end of row. Complete thumb as directed below. *Size Adult's M only:* P1, P2tog, K1, P1, K1, P2tog, P1, P2tog, [K1, P1] twice, P2tog, P1.			
Row 3: *Size Adult's M only:* P1, K1, P1, K2tog, P1, K1, P1, K2tog, [P1, K1] twice. You will have 12 sts.			
Break yarn, leaving a 12–14" tail. With a yarn needle, thread remaining sts onto the yarn tail, starting at the opposite end of the row. Thread yarn end through again, and pull firmly to close. Use yarn tail to sew side seam on thumb as on hand.			
FINISHING			
Draw all tails inside mitten. Turn mitten inside out and darn all loose ends into back of fabric. Make a second mitten following the same instructions.			

Stitching the Side Seam

To sew up the side of your Fisherman's Rib mitten so it is invisible, lay the right side edges against each other and stitch back and forth through the line of stitches along the edge of the mitten but *only* through the loop on the far side (from the edge) of each stitch. The seam should look like a line of ordinary knit stitches.

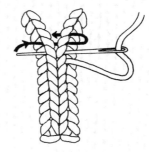

Wristers

Wristers are also called "fingerless gloves," "pulse warmers," or "half-handers," which explains their shape and function. If the wrist and palm are warm, body heat maintains the fingers in mild cold. Wristers are also worn under mittens or over gloves. These are made of angora (see list below) to be worn in a chilly house. For outdoor work or sports, use a medium-weight wool that will provide the correct gauge.

Sizes

Child's 4–6 years, Adult's medium, Adult's large

Yarn

Classic Elite, sport weight, 50% angora/50% wool

mc: 1–2 skeins purple (#4457)

cc: 1 skein lime green (#4450)

Needles

One set #6 (4mm) dp needles, *or size you need to knit correct gauge*

One set #2 (2.25mm) dp needles, for ribbing

Gauge

5½ sts = 1" (2.5cm) on larger needles in Salt and Pepper pattern

Other supplies

Stitch holder, stitch marker

cc = contrast color ◆ **dp** = double point ◆ **inc** = increase/increasing ◆ **K** = knit
K2tog = knit 2 together
M1 = make one ◆ **mc** = main color ◆ **P** = purl ◆ **st(s)** = stitch(es) ◆ **St st** = stockinette stitch ◆ **tog** = together

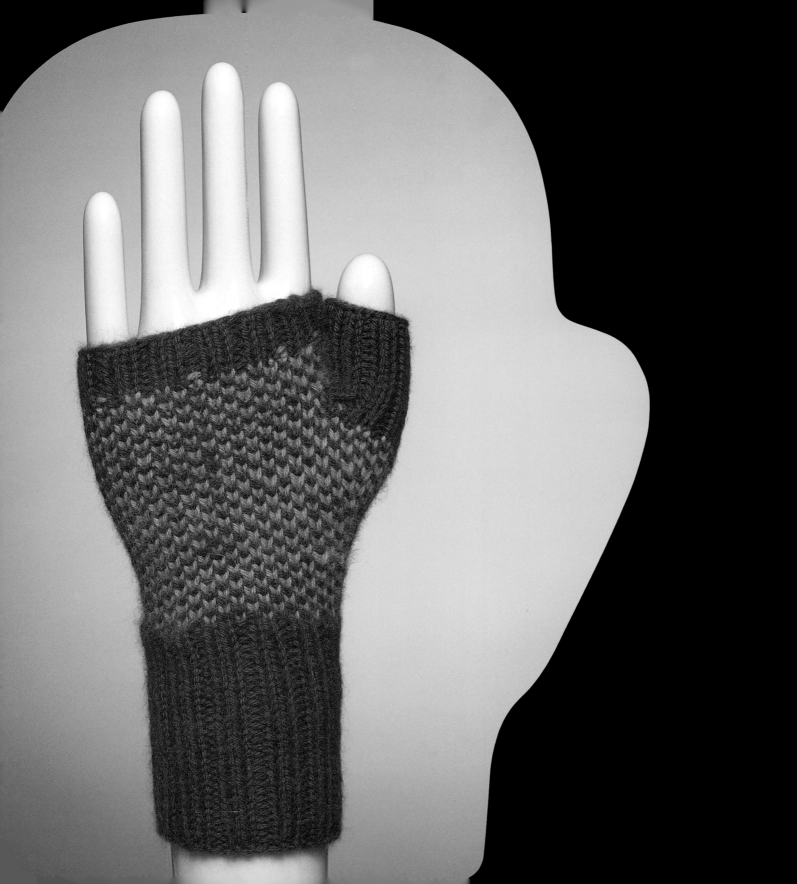

SIZES	4–6 YRS	ADULT'S M	ADULT'S L
Hand length	4½"	7½"	9"
Thumb length	1½"	2½"	3"
Hand circumference, above knuckles, including thumb tip	6"	8–9"	9½"
Finished wrister length (from cast-on edge to base of little finger)	5"	8"	9–9½"
Finished wrister width	3⅛"	3¾"	4½"
RIBBING THE CUFF			
Using smaller needles and mc, cast on	33 sts	45 sts	54 sts
Distribute sts on three dp needles: On Needle 1: On Needle 2: On Needle 3:	9 sts 12 sts 12 sts	15 sts 15 sts 15 sts	18 sts 18 sts 18 sts
Join in rnd, being careful not to twist sts. Use cast-on tail to identify beginning of rnd.			
With mc, *K2, P1; repeat from * to end of rnd for ribbing. Repeat this rnd	6 more times	6 more times	13 more times
Do not break mc. Join cc at the end of final rnd.			
Next 4 Rounds: With cc, continue in K2, P1 ribbing. (Carry color not used behind work; see pages 14–15.)			
Next 2 Rounds: Rib in mc.			
Next 2 Rounds: Rib in cc.			
Next 2 Rounds: Rib in mc.			
Next 3 Rounds: Rib in cc. Do not break cc; carry to end of cuff.			
Continue ribbing in mc until length from beginning of cuff measures	2½"	3½"	4"

STARTING THE PATTERN	4–6 YRS	ADULT'S M	ADULT'S L
Change to larger needles and St st. Twist cc and mc once at beginning of rnd, and begin Salt and Pepper pattern (page 113), starting with K1 mc. Maintain pattern continuously to end of rnd. At end of rnd, M1 in pattern	0 times	0 times	1 time
You will have	33 sts	45 sts	55 sts
Round 2: Work Salt and Pepper even on all three needles.			
INCREASING FOR THE THUMB GORE			
Round 1: K1 mc, *knit both colors (cc, then mc) into next st; repeat from * 1 more time. (See "Knitting Two Colors in One," page 99.) Place marker. Knit even in pattern to end of rnd. **NOTE:** The first st on Needle 1 (K1 mc in this rnd) marks the entrance to the thumb gore. The 4 sts between it and the marker are the base of the thumb gore. The marker is the exit from the thumb gore. On Needle 1 you will have	13 sts	17 sts	20 sts
Round 2: Knit even in Salt and Pepper.			
Round 3: K1 mc, *knit both colors (cc then mc) into next st; repeat from * 3 more times. Slip marker. Knit to end of rnd in pattern. The thumb gore has 8 sts; Needle 1 has	17 sts	21 sts	24 sts
Rounds 4–6: Knit even in pattern.			
Sizes Adult's Medium and Large only: Round 7: In pattern, K1 mc, *knit both colors into next st; repeat from * 1 more time. Knit in pattern to 2 sts before marker, *knit both colors into next st; repeat from * 1 more time. Slip marker, knit to end of rnd. The thumb gore now has	8 sts	12 sts	12 sts
Size Adult's Large only: Repeat Rounds 6–7. The thumb gore has	8 sts	12 sts	16 sts

	4–6 YRS	ADULT'S M	ADULT'S L
On the three needles, you will have	39 sts	55 sts	69 sts
Work even in pattern until work above cuff measures	1½"	2½"	3"
MAKING THE THUMB HOLE			
K1 in pattern. Place on stitch holder the thumb gore sts, plus the next sts	9 sts	13 sts	17 sts
Discard the marker. Alternating mc and cc to maintain Salt and Pepper pattern, use twisted M1 (page 14) to cast on	3 sts	3 sts	3 sts
Complete Needle 1 and rnd in pattern. You will have	33 sts	45 sts	55 sts
FINISHING THE HAND			
Knit even in Salt and Pepper until length above cuff measures	2"	4"	4½–5"
With smaller needles and mc only, work K2, P1 ribbing on all three needles for ½". (*For Adult's Large,* K2tog one time to get a multiple of 3 for this ribbing.)			
Bind off firmly.			
MAKING THE THUMB			
With smaller needles and mc, pick up from stitch holder	9 sts	13 sts	17 sts
Pick up 3 sts along top of thumb hole.			
In each corner, twisting the st as you place it on the needle, pick up one side of	1 st	1 st	2 sts
You will have	14 sts	18 sts	23 sts
Round 1: *K2, P1; repeat from * to end of rnd, knitting 2 sts tog in each corner	1 time	0 times	1 time
You will have	12 sts	18 sts	21 sts

	4–6 YRS	ADULT'S M	ADULT'S L
Continue working in K2, P1 ribbing for ½", or until thumb is the same length as ribbing for upper hand.			
Cast off firmly in K2, P1 ribbing.			
FINISHING			
Draw end through last st and break yarn. Weave in loose ends on inside and trim closely. Make a second, identical wrister. These can be worn on either hand.			

SALT AND PEPPER CHART

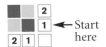 ◄— Start here

■ mc = purple

□ cc = lime green

Salt and Pepper

This pattern is a two-stitch, two-round seeding design (see chart). On an odd number of stitches knitted in the round, the shift to the next line of the pattern happens automatically (as in basket weaving) at the end of the round. Maintain the uninterrupted pattern during increases and decreases by increasing and decreasing in two-stitch units (that is, two increases or decreases side by side). Carry the darker color ahead throughout (see pages 14–15). Slipups will distort the pattern.

The first round of Salt and Pepper should begin and end with a main-color stitch. If it doesn't, check all needles (especially at the ends) for two stitches of one color together, and pull out stitches to correct the mistake. Well begun is halfway done!

North Star Mittens

Star-patterned mittens originated in Selbu, Norway, and feature a large motif on the back and Salt and Pepper seeding on the thumb and palm. This version is based on mittens from Labrador and Newfoundland, where diamonds are a popular filler motif and thumb gores are set off by contrasting lines. The mitten pictured was knit with yarn listed below; you may use any yarn that will provide the required gauge.

Sizes

Women's medium, Men's medium, Men's large

Yarn

Rauma Strikkegarn 3-ply, DK weight, 100% wool

mc: 1–2 skeins scarlet (#124)

cc: 1–2 skeins maroon (#128)

Needles

One set #2 (2.75mm) dp needles, for ribbing

One set #4 (3.5mm) dp needles, *or size you need to knit correct gauge*

Gauge

7 sts = 1" (2.5cm) on larger needles in Salt and Pepper pattern

Other supplies

12" (30cm) waste yarn, yarn needle

cc = contrast color ◆ dp = double point ◆ inc = increase/increasing ◆ K = knit ◆ K2tog = knit 2 together ◆ M1R = make 1 right-slanted increase M1L = make 1 left-slanted increase ◆ mc = main color P = purl ◆ rnd(s) = round(s) ssk2tog = slip, slip, knit 2 together ◆ st(s) = stitch(es)

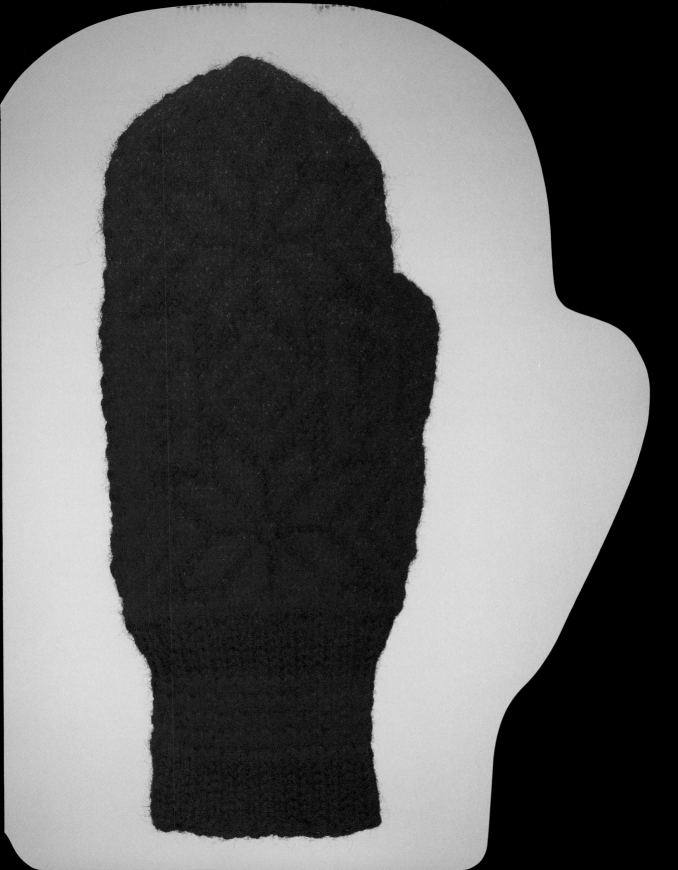

SIZES	WOMEN'S M	MEN'S M	MEN'S L
Hand length	7½"	7½"	9"
Thumb length	2½"	2½"	3"
Hand circumference, with thumb	9"	9½"	10"
Finished mitten length	10"	10"	12"
Finished mitten width	4½"	4¾"	5"
Finished thumb length	2½"	2½"	3"
RIBBING THE CUFF			
With cc and smaller needles, cast on	57 sts	60 sts	63 sts

Distribute stitches on three dp needles:
   On Needle 1:
   On Needle 2:
   On Needle 3:
	27 sts
	15 sts
	15 sts
		30 sts
		15 sts
		15 sts
			33 sts
			15 sts
			15 sts

Join in rnd, being careful not to twist sts.			
Rounds 1–6: With cc, *K2, P1; repeat from * to end of rnd.			
Rounds 7–15: Join mc. Alternate rnds of mc and cc ribbing (K2, P1). You will have 5 rnds of mc.			
Rounds 16–21: Continue K2, P1 ribbing.			
STARTING THE HAND			
Change to larger needles and stockinette stitch.			
Increase Round: In mc, M1 between the knit sts of the ribbing, evenly spaced	6 times	6 times	7 times
You will have	63 sts	66 sts	70 sts

Distribute sts on three dp needles:
   On Needle 1 (back of hand):
   On Needle 2 (palm):
   On Needle 3 (palm):
	31 sts
	16 sts
	16 sts
		35 sts
		16 sts
		15 sts
			35 sts
			18 sts
			17 sts

STARTING THE PATTERNS AND THUMB GORE (Right Mitten)	WOMEN'S M	MEN'S M	MEN'S L
NOTE: The first round is a setup round. Needle 1 (back of hand) will contain the North Star motif between vertical lines that will extend to the very tip of the mitten. Needle 2 will contain the thumb gore, outlined with cc marking sts, as well as part of the palm. Needle 3 will contain the rest of the palm sts. Both palm and thumb gore are worked in Salt and Pepper. (See pages 122–124 for patterns. Begin where indicated for your size; read from right to left.) Carry cc ahead at all times (pages 14–15).			
Round 1 Needle 1: K1 cc, K1 mc. Work Line 1 of North Star chart for desired size. Start at bottom right, and work to end of Line 1. Finish Needle 1 with K1 mc, K1 cc. Needle 2: K1 mc (marking st), work 5 sts in Salt and Pepper pattern, starting with K1 mc; K2 mc (marking sts). Knit to end of needle in Salt and Pepper. **NOTE:** The first mc st marks the entrance to the thumb gore. The 5 Salt and Pepper sts are the base of the thumb gore. The 2 mc marking sts are the exit from the thumb gore. Maintain marking sts to the thumb hole. Needle 3: Continue Salt and Pepper pattern from Needle 2 to end of needle.			
Round 2 Needle 1: K1 cc, K1 mc, work next line of North Star pattern, K1 mc, K1 cc. Needle 2: K1 mc (marking st), M1L (maintaining Salt and Pepper color sequence), K5, M1R, K2 mc, work Salt and Pepper to end of needle. (See page 89 for advice on M1L and M1R.) Needle 3: Continue in Salt and Pepper pattern to end of needle.			

	WOMEN'S M	MEN'S M	MEN'S L
Round 3 Needle 1: K1 cc, K1 mc, work next line of North Star pattern, K1 mc, K1 cc. Needle 2: K1 mc, knit in Salt and Pepper pattern to the 2 mc sts, K2 mc. Knit to end of needle in pattern. Needle 3: Knit even in Salt and Pepper pattern to end of needle.			
Repeat Rounds 2 and 3	4 more times	5 more times	6 more times
Between the marking sts on Needle 2 the thumb gore contains	15 sts	17 sts	19 sts
Knit even in patterns until work from end of cuff measures	2½"	2½"	3"
MAKING THE THUMB HOLE *(Right Mitten)*			
Round 1 Needle 1: Continue working North Star chart. Needle 2: K1 mc, place on waste yarn the thumb gore sts	15 sts	17 sts	19 sts
Maintaining Salt and Pepper color sequence and using twisted M1 (page 14), cast on 5 sts over the gap. Knit to end of needle. **NOTE:** When casting on, start with the opposite color from the st after the 2 marking sts. This allows you to fit the new sts into the pattern. Convert marking sts to Salt and Pepper as you come to them. Needle 3: Work even in pattern to end of needle. You will have	63 sts	66 sts	70 sts

Distribute sts on three dp needles:
  On Needle 1:
  On Needle 2:
  On Needle 3:
	31 sts
	16 sts
	16 sts
		35 sts
		16 sts
		15 sts
			35 sts
			18 sts
			17 sts

	WOMEN'S M	MEN'S M	MEN'S L
Knit even in patterns until you complete North Star chart	line 43	line 43	line 55

STARTING THE PATTERNS AND THUMB GORE (Right Mitten)

Round 1
Needle 1: Same as for right hand.

Needle 2: Work Salt and Pepper pattern, starting with K1 mc, to end of needle.

Needle 3: Continue from Needle 2 in Salt and Pepper pattern to the first 8 sts, K2 mc (marking sts). K5 sts in Salt and Pepper, starting with K1 mc; K1 mc (marking st).

NOTE: The first 2 mc sts mark the entrance to the thumb gore. The 5 Salt and Pepper sts form the base of the thumb gore. The last mc st marks the exit from the thumb gore. Maintain these marking sts to the thumb hole.

Round 2
Needle 1: K1 cc, K1 mc, work next line of North Start chart, K1 mc, K1 cc.

Needle 2: Work even in Salt and Pepper.

Needle 3: Work even in Salt and Pepper to first marking sts, K2 mc, M1L in Salt and Pepper, work Salt and Pepper to next marking st, M1R, K1 mc.

Round 3
Needle 1: K1 cc, K1 mc, work next line of North Star pattern, K1 mc, K1 cc.

Needle 2: Work even in Salt and Pepper.

Needle 3: Work even in Salt and Pepper to marking sts, K2 mc, work even in Salt and Pepper to marking st, K1 mc.

	WOMEN'S M	MEN'S M	MEN'S L
Repeat Rounds 2 and 3	4 more times	5 more times	6 more times

	WOMEN'S M	MEN'S M	MEN'S L
Between the marking sts on Needle 3 the thumb gore contains	15 sts	17 sts	19 sts
Knit even in patterns until work from end of cuff measures	2½"	2½"	3"

MAKING THE THUMB HOLE
(Left Mitten)

Round 1
Needle 1: Continue working North Star chart.

Needle 2: Work even in pattern.

Needle 3: Continue Salt and Pepper to the first marking sts. Convert them to Salt and Pepper. Place the thumb gore sts on a piece of waste yarn

	WOMEN'S M	MEN'S M	MEN'S L
(Round 1, Needle 3)	15 sts	17 sts	19 sts
Maintaining color sequence, use twisted M1 (page 14) to cast on 5 sts over the gap. Knit the last st (marking st), converting it to the Salt and Pepper sequence. You will have	63 sts	66 sts	70 sts
Knit even in patterns until you complete North Start chart	line 43	line 55	line 55

DECREASING THE MITTEN TIP

	WOMEN'S M	MEN'S M	MEN'S L
Distribute sts on three dp needles:			
On Needle 1:	31 sts	35 sts	35 sts
On Needle 2:	16 sts	16 sts	18 sts
On Needle 3:	16 sts	15 sts	17 sts

Round 1
Needle 1: K1 cc, ssk2tog, knit North Star motif to 3 sts from end of needle, K2tog mc, K1 cc.

Needle 2: In Salt and Pepper, K2tog, knit to end of needle.

	WOMEN'S M	MEN'S M	MEN'S L
Needle 3: In Salt and Pepper, knit to 2 sts before end of needle, ssk2tog in pattern. You will have	59 sts	62 sts	66 sts
Round 2: Knit even in patterns.			
Repeat Round 1 in	Rnds 3–8	Rnds 3–7	Rnds 3–7
You will have	35 sts	42 sts	46 sts
Next Round Needle 1: K1 cc, ssk2tog mc, K2tog mc, work chart to 5 sts before end of needle, ssk2tog mc, K2tog mc, K1 cc. Needle 2: In pattern, K2tog, work in pattern to 2 sts from end of needle, ssk2tog. Needle 3: In pattern, K2tog, knit to 2 sts from end of needle, ssk2tog in pattern. Repeat this rnd	2 more times	3 more times	3 more times
You will have	11 sts	10 sts	14 sts
Break yarn. With yarn needle, thread mc yarn end through remaining sts. Thread yarn end through remaining sts once more. Pull firmly to close. Pull both yarn ends to inside of mitten.			
MAKING THE THUMB			
Round 1: Pick up thumb gore sts from waste yarn	15 sts	17 sts	19 sts
Pick up 5 sts from the cast-on edge of the thumb hole.			
Pick up the sides of 2 sts from each corner, twisting them as you place them on the needle.			
You will have	24 sts	26 sts	28 sts

	WOMEN'S M	MEN'S M	MEN'S L
Distribute sts evenly on three dp needles, placing the beginning of the rnd at a corner. Join mc and cc. Work Salt and Pepper pattern, knitting 2 sts together on palm side of thumb one time to get to an odd number of sts. You will have	3 sts	25 sts	27 sts
Knit even in Salt and Pepper until the thumb measures	2"	2"	2½"
DECREASING THE THUMB			
Round 1: On each needle, working in pattern, K2tog, knit to last 2 sts, ssk2tog.			
Round 2: Knit even in pattern.			
Repeat Rounds 2 and 3 twice more. You will have	5 sts	7 sts	9 sts
Break yarns. With yarn needle, thread one yarn end through remaining sts. Draw yarn end though sts one more time. Pull firmly to close. Draw both ends to inside.			
FINISHING			
Turn mitten inside out and sew all tails under floats of opposite color (page 39). Trim ends close to fabric.			
Knit the other mitten. Remember to knit it for the opposite hand!			

North Star Charts

SALT AND PEPPER

2
1 ←Start here
2 1

mc = scarlet
cc = maroon

53
52
51
50
49
48
47
46
45
44
43
42
41
40
39
38
37
36
35
34
33
32
31
30
29
28
27
26
25
24
23
22
21
20
19
18
17
16
15
14
13
12
11
10
9
8
7
6
5
4
3
2
1 ← Start here

27 26 25 24 23 22 21 20 19 18 17 16 15 14 13 12 11 10 9 8 7 6 5 4 3 2 1

WOMEN'S SMALL

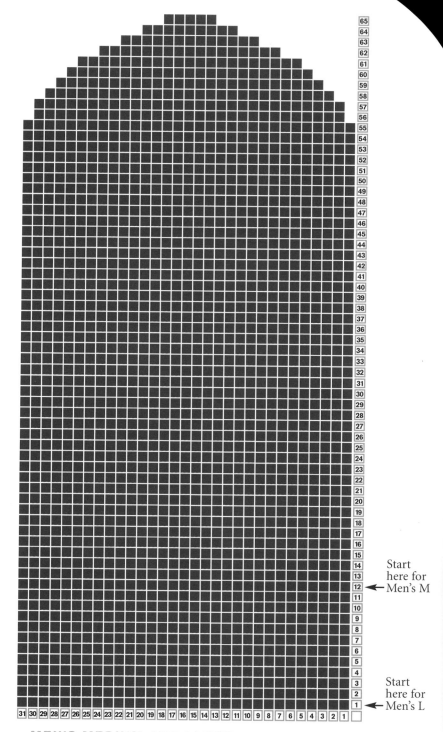

65
64
63
62
61
60
59
58
57
56
55
54
53
52
51
50
49
48
47
46
45
44
43
42
41
40
39
38
37
36
35
34
33
32
31
30
29
28
27
26
25
24
23
22
21
20
19
18
17
16
15
14
13
12 ← Start here for Men's M
11
10
9
8
7
6
5
4
3
2
1 ← Start here for Men's L

31 30 29 28 27 26 25 24 23 22 21 20 19 18 17 16 15 14 13 12 11 10 9 8 7 6 5 4 3 2 1

MEN'S MEDIUM AND LARGE

Acknowledgments

Many thanks to Nora Johnson of Five Islands, Maine, for teaching me to carry one color ahead and for helping me with mittens over many years; Janetta Dexter of Novia Scotia, for sharing her collection of traditional mittens and for teaching me two-handed knitting; Judy McGrath of Labrador, for giving me an Inuit North Star mitten; my mother-in-law, Lillemor Orm Hansen, of Rungsted, Denmark, for both the striped and the garter stitch mittens; Harriet Pardy Martin and her daughter Doris Saunders of Happy Valley, Labrador, for sharing directions for finger mitts; Torbjørg Gauslaa, for teaching me to spit splice; Meg Swanson, for her endless encouragement through thick and thin; Elizabeth Zimmerman, for teaching me the concept of proportional design; and all the unknown knitters in Brunswick, Maine, Nepal, Labrador, Newfoundland, and Norway, whose mittens came to me from a distance without names — I wish I could thank you in person. In addition, grateful thanks to Hanne Orm Tierney, Mary Ellen Czerniak, Ruth Freesia, Barbara Elkins, Dori Betjemann, Chris Hammel, Linda Burt, Cynthia Merkin, and Linda Daniels, who helped make the projects for this book and offered invaluable advice. Thanks to Russell Pierce of Bartlettyarns and Deborah Vadnais Gremlitz of Nordic Fiber Arts. And to my family, for their patience during the writing of this book, especially my daughter Hanne Orm Tierney, for her tireless knitting and checking of all the sizes and several mittens and for cheering me on and on. Also, thanks to Gwen Steege and Karen Levy at Storey Books, who worked in, on, and through all the patterns and the entire book, each with her own expertise, until these mittens were truly the best we can offer.

SUPPLIERS

Bartlettyarns, Inc.
20 Water Street
Harmony, ME 04942
Tel: (207) 683-2251
www.bartlettyarns.com

Brown Sheep Company
100662 County Road 16
Mitchell, NE 69357
Tel: (800) 826-9136
www.brownsheep.com

Classic Elite Yarns
300A Jackson Street
Lowell, MA 01852
Tel: (800) 444-5648

The Naked Sheep
493 Main Street
Bennington, VT 05201
Tel: (877) 917-4337
www.nakedsheep.com

Nordic Fiber Arts
4 Cutts Road
Durham, NH 03824
Tel: (603) 868-1196
www.nordicfiberarts.com

Northampton Wools
11 Pleasant Street
Northampton, MA 01060
Tel: (413) 586-4331

Peace Fleece
475 Porterfield Road
Porter, ME 04068
Tel: (800) 482-2841
www.peacefleece.com

WEBS
Service Center Road
Northampton, MA 01061
Tel: (800) 367-9327
www.yarn.com/webs/

Index

Note: Page numbers for charts are in **bold;** those for photos and illustrations are in *italics.*

Adults' mittens, sizing, 8–9
Anchoring floats, 39
Antique baby mittens, 70

Canadian size needles, **6**
Carrying colors, 15, *15*
Casting on, 10, *10*
Chicky Feet Mittens, 34–39, *35,* **36–39**
Children's mittens, sizing, 8–9
Chipman's Block, 62–69, *63,* **64–69,** *69*
Color (multi) knitting, 5, 12, *12,* 13,
    14–15, *15,* 39, 69, *69,* 76, 99, *99,*
    113
Conversion chart for needles, **6**
Counted-stitch embroidery cuffs, 27,
    27
Covered with Colors, 78–85, *79,*
    80–85
Cuffs, embroidered, 27, *27*

Decreasing, *26,* 26–27, **26–27**
Dexter, Janetta, 62
Diamonds, Labrador, 92–99, *93,*
    94–99
Double knitting, 15, *15*
Double-point needles, 6, **6,** 11, *11*
Dyeing, Kool-Aid, 21
Dye lots of yarn, 5

Embroidered cuffs, 27, *27*

Fair Isle, 15
Fingerless gloves, 108–13, *109,* **110–13**
Finger Mitts, Skier's, 52–61, *53,* **54–61**
Fisherman's Rib, 100–107, *101,* **102–7,**
    103–4, 107

Fitting (sizing) mittens, 8–9
Fleur-de-Lis Mittens, 40–45, *41,* **42–45**
Floats, anchoring, 39
Fulled mittens, 5, 22, 46, 51

Garter stitch mittens, 28–33, *29,*
    30–33
Gauge (tension), 5, 7, *7*

Half-handers, 108–13, *109,* **110–13**
Hand, measuring, 8–9
Hanks (yarn), 33
Hansen, Lillemor Orm, 28

Increasing, 12–13, 73, *73,* 89, *89,* 99,
    99, 104, *104,* 113

Jacquard, 15
Joining new yarn, 11–12, *11–12*

K2tog (knit two together), 26, *26*
Kids' Fulled Mittens, 46–51, *47,* **48–51**
Knitting, 4–15
    carrying colors, 15, *15*
    casting on, 10, *10*
    color (multi), 5, 12, *12,* 13, 14–15,
        15, 39, 69, *69,* 76, 99, *99,* 113
    decreasing, *26,* 26–27, **26–27**
    double knitting, 15, *15*
    double-point needles, 6, **6,** 11, *11*
    floats, anchoring, 39
    fulled mittens, 5, 22, 46, 51
    hand, measuring, 8–9
    increasing, 12–13, 73, *73,* 89, *89,* 99,
        99, 104, *104,* 113
    joining new yarn, 11–12, *11–12*

needles, 6, **6**, 11, *11*
shaping, 12–14, *14*
side seam stitching, 107, *107*
sizing (fitting) mittens, 8–9
splicing new yarn, 11, *11*
starting, 4
tension (gauge, stitch gauge), 5, 7, *7*
thumbs (thumbies), 8, 9, 12–13
twisted make one (twisted M1),
    13–14, *14*
waste yarn, knitting on, 45, *45*
weaving in, 12, *12*, 39
yarns, 5, 33
Knitting in the round, 6, 11, *11*
Knitting kit, contents of, 8
Kool-Aid dyeing, 21

Labrador Diamonds, 92–99, *93*,
    94–99
Lillemor's Mittens, 28–33, *29*, **30–33**

M1L/M1R (make one with left/right
    slant), 89, *89*
M1 (make one), 13
Maine cast-on, 10, *10*
Martin, Harriet Pardy, 52
Multicolor knitting, 5, 12, *12*, 13,
    14–15, *15*, 39, 69, *69*, 76, 99, *99*,
    113

Needles, 6, **6**, 11, *11*
Nepalese Mittens, 86–91, *87*, **88**, *89*,
    90–91
North Star Mittens, 114–24, *115*,
    116–24

Peek-a-Boo Mittens, 70–77, *71*,
    72–77
Pinch room, 9
Polar Bear Mitts, 22–27, *23*, **24–27**,
    26–27
Pull skeins, 33
Pulse warmers, 108–13, *109*, **110–13**

Ribbing, 7

Salt and Pepper, 61, **61**, 69, **69**, 99, **99**,
    113, **113, 122–24**
Selbu mittens, 114
Shaping, 12–14, *14*
Side seam stitching, 107, *107*
Sizing (fitting) mittens, 8–9
Skier's Finger Mitts, 52–61, *53*, **54–61**
Splicing new yarn, 11, *11*
Ssk2tog (slip, slip, knit two together),
    26, *26*
Star-patterned mittens, 114–24, *115*,
    116–24
Starting knitting, 4
Stitch gauge (tension), 5, 7, *7*
Stockinette, 7
Stop-and-Go Mittens, 16–20, *17*,
    18–20
Stranding, 15, 39
Striped mittens, 16–20, *17*, **18–20**
Substituting yarn, 5
Synthetic mittens, 5

Tension (gauge, stitch gauge), 5, 7, *7*
Test swatch, 7
Thumbs (thumbies), 8, 9, 12–13
Trompe de l'oeil checkerboards, 92
Twisted make one (twisted M1),
    13–14, *14*
Two-for-one increase, 13, 73, *73*

US/UK size needles, **6**

Waste yarn, knitting on, 45, *45*
Weaving in, 12, *12*, 39
Wool, 5
Wristers, 108–13, *109*, **110–13**

Yarns, 5, 33

Zimmermann, Elizabeth, 13

another Storey title you might enjoy:

knit hats!

15 Cool Patterns to Keep You Warm

Edited by GWEN STEEGE

Hardcover
ISBN 1-58017-482-5
Full-color photographs and
illustrations throughout
96 pages
Available wherever books are sold.

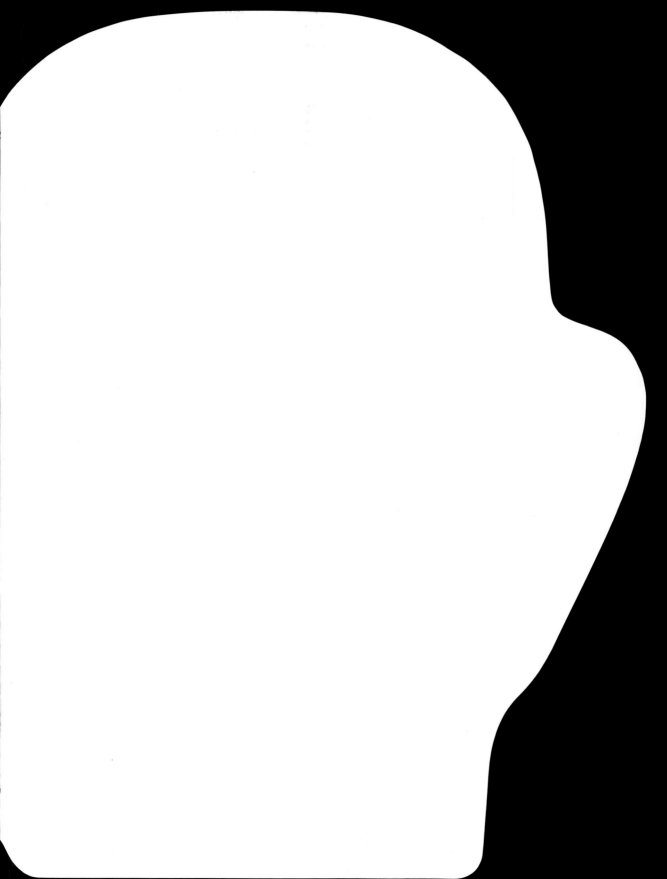